TIGER
CLAW &
VELVET
PAW

TIGER
CLAW &
VELVET
PAW

Malee

TRANSLATED BY
YEHUDA SHAPIRO

Arlington Books
King Street, St. James's
London

TIGER CLAW AND VELVET PAW
first published May 1986 by
Arlington Books (Publishers) Ltd
15–17 King Street St. James's
London SW1

© *1984 Verlag Simon & Magiera KG, München*
English translation © *Arlington Books 1986*

Typeset in England by
Inforum Ltd, Portsmouth
Printed and bound in England by
Billing and Sons Ltd,
Worcester

British Library Cataloguing in Publication Data
Malee
Tiger claw, velvet paw
1. Prostitution
I. Title. II. Tiger kralle und
Samtpfote. English
306.7'42'0924 HQ117

ISBN 0–85140–684–X

Foreword by Malee

After the typhoon had blown its cocoon away the butterfly began to spread its wings

I would have liked to put this beautiful and flattering image at the head of the story of my life until now, but a title needs to be shorter and more gripping.

I am happy and rather proud that Julia Berlinghausen and Soavanee Theeravit thought my story worth writing down. Left to my own devices I would have waited until I reached the Sea of Tranquility. But we have used the still at the eye of the storm to reconstruct this story with the written word.

It is based on entries in my diary, memories I had put down in writing, and also some letters which never reached their destination and were returned to me; Soavanee has translated all these from the Thai. Then Julia and Soavanee have written down what they have remembered of our long conversations together, and I am so grateful for the empathy they have felt with my story. I have been able to trust my "ghostwriters", who have put all the fragments of my memories together and made a narrative of them.

As the reader will see from the later chapters of this book, I am now at home with the German language, because being able to speak the language in a foreign country is the best way of asserting yourself. But someone was needed to express my reminiscences, thoughts and images in a more elegant and literary German. For this, I proffer a sprig of lotus to Julia Berlinghausen.

Reading the complete manuscript I noticed that the inner growth of the narrator is very strongly portrayed. She likes looking ahead and bringing forward events which happened later. This has occurred because I was finding my way in and between such different worlds, and the various experiences often run into one another. The persona can only remain constant and detached in a few of the narrative passages.

Another aspect of this is the way many of the images, similes and thoughts in the first three chapters of the book go beyond the range of my perceptions at the time. Some western influences have found their way into this evocation of the past. They are an inevitable consequence of my contact with a new world and my expanded and altered experience. But I very much hope that those first three chapters will be the ones to show the reader how far Malee, the little daughter of a rice farmer, has come.

Foreword by Julia Berlinghausen

The world of a brothel
How we met Malee

The first time we saw Malee everything about her was completely in keeping with the personality and intentions we discovered so much more about later.

I was sitting with my friend Soavanee in an Italian restaurant in Hamburg, drinking a Campari and soda. Soavanee was telling me what she had planned to do once she had finished her studies. I could not help feeling a sense of concern and responsibility when she told me about her doubts over whether to spend another two years here to fulfil some of her career ambitions. The way she expressed herself was restrained because she did not want to "lose face", but she was obviously so homesick that it was affecting her physically. She was quite open about her dislike of the aggressive social habits here, particularly the gross lack of consideration for foreigners, and above all the rude way attentions are often forced upon Asian women.

Then Malee walked in.

We could not see her yet, but the effect she had was evident on the faces of the men around us. Of course, the Italian waiters were the first to turn their heads; it is in their temperament and it suits the image of the Latin lover that they cultivate. But then the ears of the obviously intellectual man diagonally opposite began to glow alarmingly. This forty-year old with the thinning hair and compensatory beard suddenly interrupted his flow of conversation. If his eloquence had been acting as some kind of sexual substitute it obviously did not need to any more.

There is no doubt that Malee is beautiful. Her cat-like slanting eyes, her long and shiny black hair, her wavy lips with their delicate purplish tint at the edges, her silky skin and her slim, lissome body encapsulate every possible cliché about the seductive oriental woman. A she-tiger with velvet paws. And you would have thought that she was just looking to perpetuate these clichés. But, knowing something about male fantasies, it seemed to me that she was out to drive men to sensual distraction.

She was wearing skintight nappa-leather trousers which clung to the lines of her buttocks and lay like a second skin over her vulva. Her short high-heeled boots made her legs seem almost as long as those of Dali's Fire figure. She was wearing a shiny black satin blouse, with wide sleeves and a deep décolletage. As she moved you inevitably caught sight of her small firm breasts with their large dark nipples. She had casually thrown on a shawl in imitation tiger skin. It was quite obvious that she was not afraid to look sexy. She even seemed like a radiantly erotic, but uninvolved, dominatrix. She was sensual in a casual, almost dreamy way which made me think of the tranquil sense of superiority of the tiger, who before man knew no natural enemy.

All the tables were full. She looked around for a moment and then asked us if we had a spare place at ours. I was expecting her voice to be darkly vibrant, and it was. She ordered scampi, perhaps to remind herself of the *gung* that is considered such a delicacy in Thailand – if you can afford it. We gradually got talking, and I was surprised by the quality of her German, which was cultured, rich in imagery, and even surprisingly literary. This was nothing like the pidgin language which the Thai prostitutes here usually use.

I must confess that I had no doubts as to her line of business, and since then I have often wondered about my own "moral" attitude towards it; in my braver moments I have even thought that I may be jealous because I would never dare be so openly provocative in public. But I have come to realise that this behaviour is "merchandising", the exploitation of natural resources of sexuality in a male-dominated world. Soavanee seemed to be even more amazed by Malee than I was. Soavanee comes from a well-off family, and so has been able to study over here. Her father owns an import and export company. Hesitatingly, she has also hinted that he has a hand in the Golden Triangle, the opium and heroin trade. But business is one thing, the traditional Buddhist morality of a wealthy family is another. Soavanee is open-minded and soci-ally-aware, but she really did not know what to think when she met a prostitute from her own country.

Yet our uncertainty soon changed to sympathy and empathy when Malee told us about her life, opening the Pandora's box of her experiences on many occasions when we later met as friends. Our sympathy was not a matter of feeling sorry for her. We were able to learn from her. We were two women from very far apart and differing cultures, while she was a prostitute who had moved between these two worlds and she showed us how a woman's body could so easily not be her own, at the same time making it clear to us what it is to be a woman, and to be more specifically in the privileged position of not being a prostitute.

Malee had a magical galvanising effect on us. All our petty restraints about recognising ourselves as self-confident bourgeois women in an apparently secure position went up in smoke. And from the ashes there arose a new realisation: that no-one can be certain of living their life in a socially secure position, confident of human solidarity. And women especially must be aware that they are the first to be sacrificed in times of war and economic need. We of the affluent society must not forget that poor countries far away are subject to colonialist influences, whether direct or indirect. And the invasion of these countries finds its clearest expression in the way women are forced to prostitute themselves to the tourists, sometimes even while they are still children.

And Malee was doing her utmost to combat this by asserting herself using every method known to women. To escape from being the sacrificial victim, she appeared to take on the role of the victim, becoming instead the priestess at the ceremony. She became the Babylonian temple whore, ready to take on anyone; a siren with spell-binding erotic powers, exercised with a cold and alienating aesthetic which just served to heighten desire. She is the sorceress of our age, an outcast caught between cultures and homelands, a camp-follower between the armies of the male world.

She both reconciles and exaggerates contradictions. She represents the elemental mother-figure, who, though physically debased and defiled, remains unspoiled and able to offer hope.

And she has pity for men, who in their depraved dreams of freedom see themselves as knights errant, making conquests in the intervals between their stultifying work. It is revealing to learn that German industrial workers are among the most sex-hungry tourists in the popular tropical resorts.

Malee, the prostitute, has not taught us that relations between men and women are so hostile as to be beyond repair. No, the strength she has retained through all she has experienced represents the hope that freedom and equality may be gained by exploring further the ancient and mythical sexual relationship between woman and man.

Dreams of the Bamboo Grove

My thoughts wander back

I feel especially cold in the late autumn and early spring when the days are wet and chilly. I am overwhelmed by greyness. Everything is grey: the plaster on the walls, the concrete, the sky, the tarmac, the sheets of rain, the shapes of people and vehicles, the silhouettes of the few trees to be seen. I brace myself against the Western city cold. My head is filled with melancholy thoughts, and I want to get up and go somewhere else. I feel a nostalgic longing for the distant homeland of my childhood, yet it has now become almost foreign to me. As I turn to look at the pot-plants and decorative palms in my flat, I wish myself back in time.

I would like to hear the whispering and rustling of the bamboo grove, see the wind rippling through the fields of green rice-shoots, and listen to the monsoon rain in the evening as it splashes on the vault of leaves overhead . . . When I go to throw another helping of swill to the pig which lives between the teak stilts of our house, I secure my *patung* with a knot at my chest and run through the pouring rain, laughing as I go. Then my brothers and sisters giggle and call me "ruffled chicken" or "shivering hound". Our mother gives us rice in fish sauce and bakes us fish which my brothers and sisters catch in baskets in the flooded paddy fields. We talk, joke and play until the night overtakes us and sends us to bed on our mattresses of rice-straw. After a period of deep sleep I dream happily of Lek. He is fifteen and lives in the next village. Lithe, slim and muscular, he has a smile in his eyes as well as on his lips. In his quiet way he lets me know that he desires me, that his body is filled with impatient and wilful urges. In the evening I bathe at the pool of the little stream, which is our public bath-house. Sometimes I hear a quiet rustling. The hairs on the back of my neck stand on end with strange excitement. I do not have to see him to know that Lek is hiding in the bushes. Now the hair on my head prickles too. In a daze, I open my *patung*, uncovering nipples hardened from the cool water. As I unwind the cloth I stretch myself, knowing that he must be able to see me. The thought of this excites me too. As I return home by way of the mule-track my whole body is throbbing. I am finding out what it is to be a woman and am filled with joyful curiosity.

I am now dreaming the ancient dream. The excitement is past, and now my womb is filled with the seed of posterity, the hopeful image of my own transience. We follow the eternal path: we are rice farmers and plant anew. We are performing the ancient ceremony, sowing rice, catching fish, spinning sisal, weaving cloth, feeding pigs, chickens and ducks. We keep the strong and silent water buffalo, who plough and harrow our fields, and thresh the rice.

This is the dream that in past times became a reality and was constantly renewed.

★

How distant I am now from the life of my ancestors. This distance cannot be measured in kilometres or degrees. I have lost my sense of security. I can no longer survey my environment. My special identity as a woman no longer exists. I have been cast adrift in an unknown universe.

I recall the stories told by my grandmother. In them she harked back to the traditions of her grandmother and great-grandmother. The old way of life in Thailand ran a steady and peaceful course. The cultivation of rice set the rhythm of the peasant's work. Social life revolved around the temple, where we expressed our feelings of joy and sorrow, where we tried to find answers to our questions on the meaning of existence, where we learned, where mysticism and enlightenment were to be found. It was the men who governed, but the women were the ones who determined the course of social and economic affairs in the self-sufficient village community. They decided when to transplant the rice, and when the men should take the water buffalo to plough and thresh. They took the surplus produce to the markets of the *changwat*, the province, spreading knowledge and information beyond the confines of our village and bringing news to the community.

Even while I was living in my village in Isan, the north-eastern part of Thailand, I sensed that the security of the centuries-old peasant tradition was threatened. I could see this in the worried faces of my parents and other adults, and in the satisfied smiles of the Chinese purchasers and millers. They told me more than any explanation of the economic background could have done.

Never again would I see the play of light in the bamboo grove of my childhood.

13

Bitter Rice

Awakening

The red earth of the Isan was still covered in darkness and the night's dew. The pig beneath the house grunted as he shifted in his sleep. The cockerel preened his feathers, but it was not yet time for him to crow.

I shivered. The sound of my mother's bare feet came closer, and she gently touched my shoulder. But I had already been awake for a long time. The fears and sorrows of the past few days were over. My dried-up eyes were burning, I had a pit in my stomach and each breath was an effort. The process of thought had become painfully physical in a way I had never known before. I splashed my face with water a few times, and my eyes found temporary relief. Then I knotted my *patung*, picked up the cloth with my few belongings in it and huddled myself up beneath the overhang of the roof.

I thought of my elder brother who, a few weeks before, had left on an even longer journey. He had gone to Bangkok as bought labour, which had meant that my parents did not have to sell the water buffalo. But the reprieve had been short-lived and now it was time for me to leave on a journey.

My father and younger brothers and sisters had gathered silently and were now squatting around me. Mother timidly

14

offered me a bowl of warm glutinous-rice soup. She looked concerned as I turned my head away and clutched my bundle. As night turned quickly to day I saw through the half-light the approaching gleam of a dust-monster's eyes.

The rattling Japanese minibus drew up sharply in front of our house. A fat Chinese leaned out from the driver's seat, and called in a loud voice:

"Off we go to fame and fortune! There's work, a future and lots of money to be had in the town."

My brothers and sisters began to sob, I hugged them and clasped my parents' hands. Then I took my bundle and ran down the steps and got in next to the Chinese in the Mazda, whose motor was still running. The dealer waved to my parents, but they just stared back without moving. He put the bus into gear and we set off along the bumpy road. I did not look back. As the bus got faster I heard another noise. It was Lek, panting wildly as he ran, trying to keep up with the vehicle, his face distorted with the strain. He choked out words to me:

"I'll work hard . . . I'll come for you . . ."

Then he stumbled, and fell to the ground with the full force of his speed. For a moment I saw him flat on the ground, then he was hidden by a cloud of dust. I broke into painful sobbing, but no tears would come.

The fat dealer turned to me and spoke loudly over the noise:

"You should be proud of being able to help your family." He grinned. "And you're a pretty girl too. There's a lot a pretty girl can do in the town."

I could smell the alcohol on his breath through the air-stream. He had probably drunk a lot of *Mekhong* whisky the night before. It turned my stomach.

The breakneck journey lasted two hours, during which the hung-over Chinese kept quiet. It was to be a long time before I saw another female water buffalo suckling her pale calf. We approached Khon Kaen, the major town of the north-east. The driver made his way confidently through a web of streets and side-streets that I found confusing. He sullenly reminded me to be hard-working and obedient in my domestic work, and told me that the master of the house was an important and powerful police officer. A little while later he stopped in front of some high garden walls with large pieces of broken glass embedded on top. The Chinese hooted and the *chaosuon*, an old gardener,hobbled up hurriedly to open the large steel gate. We entered the courtyard and were faced by an impressive stone house set partially on concrete stilts. There were buzzing monsters sitting in the windows, the air-conditioning machines; I soon came to fear them, because the constant changing from the warm humidity of the air outside and the artificial coolness in the family's rooms quickly gave me the worst and most stubborn cold of my life.

At the front door the senior maid of the household was waiting for us. She must have seen at least sixty-five New Year's Days, and wore her snow-white hair cut very short in the way of old women who have calmly renounced all vanity. Her face was wrinkled like an elephant's skin and she wore a rather worried expression, but her eyes gave me confidence with their glowing goodness and liveliness. The Chinese handed me over to this old woman and went away without saying anything. I felt a physical sense of relief. Having taken off my rubber sandals I went through the doorway onto the cool tiles of the entrance hall. The chill made my muscles go stiff and my hair stand on end. The old woman smiled:

"You'll get used to it. It's not like in the old days."

She led the way. Her back was bent from years of service, and she could not have been tall enough to look her masters in the eye, even if they were seated at table. I followed her up a curved staircase to a gallery; it overlooked the general living area which was divided into different levels. Behind a heavy rosewood desk sat the mistress. I approached her bowing and only raised my eyes when she asked me in a stern voice to tell her my name and where I came from.

"Things will be good for you here if you are hard-working and obedient. If you are, we will keep you on after the first year and you will even be able to visit your family for two days. I will give you ten *baht* pocket money for the first month and you will also get a blouse and a *patung*. Auntie will tell you the rest."

The old woman, known to me as Auntie from then on, led me back to the front door. We went through the outer door, which had a mosquito net stretched across it, and as it shut behind me I felt warm, damp air all around me, and my body could relax again. Auntie showed me the way to the domestic quarters of the building. They were attached to the rear facade of the house and, surprisingly, were built traditionally out of wood – perhaps the master's parents had lived there. The kitchen and laundry-room were on the ground floor and the servants' bedrooms were upstairs. Auntie showed me a little room which had nothing in it but a straw mattress. When I had undone my bundle she explained to me who else was on the staff: her husband who was the gardener, the chauffeur, and his young wife, who looked after the cleaning. My duties were to be the care of the laundry, helping in the kitchen and at table, and washing up.

Auntie must have realised how tense and scared I felt.

"You don't have to be afraid of the mistress. She is severe and moody because she is not a well woman. She hardly ever beats you, though. The children only come home during the holidays – they are students at the Chulalongkon University in Bangkok. And the master . . . you only have to be careful of him when he's drunk too much. Then he is possessed by an evil spirit. I've got a little amulet for you here. That will protect you."

She then showed me my duties. She was pleased to see that I was quick to learn and good with my hands. Her kindness was like a fire which gradually began to warm away the numb

feeling inside me. When the cicadas began their nightly con-
cert and the stray cats yowled in the darkness I fell onto my
mattress, undid my *patung* and fell immediately into a dream-
less exhausted sleep.

★

In the days that followed my life began to take a regular course
again, becoming predictable and ordinary. Of course, the
terrible anxiety I had felt for the first time in my life did not
disappear altogether, but it was sent back to the kingdom of
evil spirits. Nightmares gave way to the surging strength of
my vital young woman's body and its instinct for survival.

We servants got on well with each other, forming a close-
knit community. Privately we begrudged our defenceless
servitude. Without saying anything openly, we expressed
such feelings in little plays on words and humorous asides. In
the evening we often sat together and told each other about
our villages, about the communal festivals in the temples,
about cock-fights and buffalo-fights and other things we
enjoyed. I even managed to make myself write a long letter to
my family by the flickering light of a candle stub. In it, I tried
to stop them from worrying and mentioned that it would not
even be a year before we saw each other again.

I only ever saw the master of the house in the evening. His
breakfast every morning seemed to consist of one or two
bottles of *nam soda* (soda water), and he ate his lunch at the
canteen or a restaurant, so I only saw him when I took in
dinner or cleared the table. His stomach was like an overripe
durian fruit, but he only ate very small portions of Auntie's
delicious food (I knew it tasted good because I used to pick at
it). He seemed to fill himself up with endless pint bottles of
singha beer and with whisky. Except when he was giving me

orders he took hardly any notice of me, but I sometimes caught him looking at me furtively. I was disturbed by these looks from his red eyes. He kept his head down and raised them towards me, like a fighting buffalo who seems to be at rest but is really getting ready for the attack. But I felt safe in the new reality of my work, and put all thoughts of danger from my mind.

★

It was now only in the moments before I fell asleep that I really thought longingly of my family and village and dreamed of Lek. My duties and Auntie's kindness gave me other things to think about.

The rainy season was approaching, so the mistress had decided to go off while there was still time to Nongkhai, where the family had a country house on the shores of the Mekong across from Vientiane. The chauffeur and his wife had gone with her, and on one particular Saturday evening Auntie and her husband had been given leave to go and celebrate the birth of a great-grandchild. This meant that I was the only servant at the master's disposal. The monsoon was heralded by an oppressive humidity which, combined with the heat, caused a gleaming layer of sweat to form on the skin. My white blouse clung damply to my body and had become transparent. The sultry air was filled with the croaking of frogs in the nearby pond.

I walked through a haze of dampness to the house. The sudden cold of the air-conditioning made my nipples thrust against the moist material. The master had called from his bedroom. I knocked at his door and walked cautiously in. The room smelled of stale smoke and alcohol even though the air-conditioning was working. The master was standing in front of me with a glass of whisky in his hand, swaying slightly. Although the room was unnaturally cold the bare flesh of his fatty torso was covered in sweat. All he had on was a silk *ganggeng*, the white wrap-round breeches of the southern fishermen. I was very frightened, but this did not stop me from noticing how his loose lips were glistening wet with drink, and that his eyes were narrowed like a cat's. It turned into a bad dream. I tried to escape him, but my legs became weak. They would not obey my will. It was as if I were following a heady, sickly-sweet scent of corruption. Yet I knew with a terrible clarity that I had come to a crossroads in my life.

His voice was hoarse and his words came out disjointedly.

"You are not showing proper respect. Why aren't you bowing your head in my presence? I ought to punish you. You know that nobody may oppose me. But I'm good to you because you are a pretty little hummingbird. I'm going to give you something, and if you're a good girl you might even get something more."

He came close to me, ripped the top button from my blouse and stuck a crumpled hundred-baht note down my front. He grinned stupidly, in anticipation of his success.

He did not expect any resistance from me. And why should he have? He was the most powerful man around, and his word was law. He could be swayed by bribery, but not by a girl who was hardly more than a child attempting to assert herself. I was frozen with fear. But I knew that I must try and protect myself. I wanted to be like the bamboo which bends in the wind and rises again. But the bamboo can be felled by an axe.

I risked a desperate leap towards the door, but he reacted with surprising speed and agility for such a fat man. Driven by lust and anger he pounced on me with such force that I fell to the ground, knocking myself out on the stone floor.

I came back halfway to reality from somewhere very far away. Scraps of memory and foreboding, dull pain and crazy dreams swirled in a haze around me. Fear finally triumphed, the fear that I would never get back to the real world.

It was as if my body had been torn to pieces. My arms and legs were one great bluish bruise. My head was a balloon on the end of a string. My hymen was torn and my anus was sore. I heard a noise which brought me closer to consciousness. It was familiar, yet it terrified me. I was puzzled for a moment before I realised what it was. A man was lying next to me. A fat, ugly man who was snoring. After all that had happened all he could do was *snore*.

I opened my eyes and tried to make sense of my situation. My *patung* and blouse were on the floor beside the bed. The blouse was torn, the *patung* was stained with blood. In my navel lay the crumpled banknote. There was a sticky tightness in my pubic hair and between my legs. I wondered what it could be, and was overcome with revulsion when I realised it was dried-up semen. Yet I was moved to action too.

As if I was not really awake I sat up, shook off the dizziness and reached for my skirt and blouse. I stopped for a moment and wondered whether to take the money. Eventually I did, driven by the same instinct that prevented me from so much as looking at the man. He was driven from my memory. I had to survive, I had to get away.

I left the house cautiously, but with a sense of determination. My groin felt like an open wound, but I could not let that bother me. Only when the garden gate shut behind me did I realise that the monsoon had come. The heavy rain was streaming around me. In no time my hair and clothes were soaking wet. As I walked through the darkness I felt the encrustations of blood and semen loosen and run down the inside of my legs. I had to rush behind a bush to empty my bowels. A little further on I threw up. The rain washed everything away, showering and cleansing me. Each painful step took me further from the house, nearer to my unknown goal.

I made my way barefoot through the streets, knee-deep in flood water. Sheets of rain fell before me, my sodden hair was hanging over my face and the streets around me were pitch-black. All I knew was that I was making my way through the gurgling rush of water, moving against the flow.

Several times I stumbled into invisible potholes and had to use what strength I had left to pull myself out of the torrent. It was exhausting and the path seemed never-ending. A strange feeling overcame me as if I heard the melodious sound of sweet voices, telling me how easy it would be just to fall, to be carried down to the Mekong, over the crashing Khone falls, across the delta and into the wide ocean. But I groped my way onwards. I suddenly caught sight of some lights to my left. They were at different levels, shining intermittently through the curtain of rain. I gathered my thoughts together.

This must be the *kosa* hotel, the only place where so many lights would be on at this time of night. That meant that a row of old wooden buildings must be on my right, with a restaurant, a bar and a hotel.

There was no strength or willpower left in me. As I turned to the right I noticed that the water was falling more slowly. I was down on all fours, searching for the wall of a building. I eventually came up against a stone step and dragged myself up two more steps and out of the water. My fingers felt the wood of a door. I pushed down the handle and the door opened to show a flight of steps leading up to a dim red light, which seemed to me like the glow of dawn after a long dark nightmare. I closed the door and began to climb the stairs. A few steps up my ankle gave way beneath me and I crashed down the flight, collapsing like a broken doll at the bottom. I looked in numb amazement at the ankle as it swelled up. The sound of excited female voices came to me from above. They came closer until I saw a face next to me. It was covered with make-up and smelled strongly of perfume, but it expressed great warmth and concern.

"You poor little thing. What are you doing here?"

Before I could answer I felt feminine hands picking me up to carry me upstairs. They kindly removed my dripping clothes, rubbed my wet skin and wrapped a *pakomah* round my head like a turban. Tea was poured into my mouth. I was being asked many questions, and though I tried to answer them my responses came out in the wrong order. I strung scraps of words together at a mad rush, but the world was slipping away into delirious fantasy. All I could hear was the voice that belonged to the first face I had seen.

"Put her in my bed. What she needs is rest, not all your stupid talk."

★

The spirits of delirium which had held me captive for days in their dark kingdom had disappeared. Strength was beginning to pulse once more through my veins, driven on by my will to survive. I can imagine nothing better than the feeling of taking hold of yourself after a time of fear, transforming your pain into strength, exchanging nightmares for firm reality.

My amazement at finding out where I was being sheltered soon turned into curiosity. The first face I saw belonged to Noi, a *mama-san*, the madame of a brothel. Those hands which had helped me were practised in a craft I had first heard about from drunken men in my village as they talked laughingly of visits to the city. The priest in our *wad* (temple) had hinted darkly at it as a distant but powerful threat to morals. And here I was surrounded by a flock of these birds of paradise who were meant to be so dangerous.

It was a strange new world to me.

I was fascinated by the girls and women around me. I had never worn make-up in my life, and only knew of the red dye

23

left on your lips from chewing beetle-nuts. But my new friends were never without make-up. They wore it both day and night to lighten their skin. Their lips were painted with bright red *lipastick*, as if they wanted their mouths to look like flowers bursting into bloom. Some of them even wore long false eyelashes. They mostly wore their hair long and loose.

But when they were asleep, and when they got up in the morning, they looked like death-masks, since their skin was covered in a thick layer of powder which was supposed to be protective. Their hair would be put up in a comfortable style and they wore a simple *patung* instead of the striking clothes which made such an impression on me. They mostly had very short frilly nylon dresses in garish colours like red, pink, orange and lime green, and tottered around on high heels. Some of them had a "shady" image and wore cutaway tops in black silk, leather skirts up to their crotch and knee-high patent boots with fold-over tops. But they only dressed like this for the room on the first floor where they met customers, and for the ground-floor bar and restaurant. In their bedrooms and elsewhere they looked like girls from the country, which is what most of them were.

The girls were unashamedly practical and vain in their attitude to their bodies and looks. After all, that was what they had to sell, that was what made them their money. I was sized up too. The girls examined my hair and declared it fine and silky. Nid, the cheeky one, kissed me on the mouth in a gesture of mock desire and stated that it was "soft and smooth as a *longan* fruit". She unwrapped my *patung*, leaving me blushing before the other girls. They giggled as she stood behind me, her hands cupped over my breasts, and said jokingly:

"Not as droopy as yours, Eo. Nice smooth firm little melons." She ran her hands over my stomach, buttocks and inner thighs, and grunted lasciviously. "No roughness or wrinkles like the old cows have. Her skin is lovely and fresh, like after taking a cool bath."

No-one had seen Noi come in. When she saw what Nid was doing to me she took hold of a stick of bamboo and slapped her over the feet.

"Don't you touch that girl, you filthy bitch!" she screamed. She looked daggers at me and stormed out.

Noi was jealous. When I realised this I felt a strange new sensation. What did I know about passion and jealousy? My feelings for Lek had been gentle, dreamy and detached from reality. Now I was strangely pleased to see someone driven to jealousy and anger because of me. I was no longer the victim in the human chain, and felt almost excited at the power I had in me. I had been a peasant girl brought up in the old traditions, and I had been dragged off. Now I had to find a new life to replace the old one. And all I had to offer this tough world around me was my pretty, young body and my new-found willpower. I faced up to the cruel facts of my situation, and saw that only one route was open to me.

At first, Noi's feeling towards me had simply been maternal and protective. I don't know when it was that she started wanting me. In my delirium after I arrived there I had often sensed her body, her comforting hand stroking me. As I convalesced her stroking became more playful, brushing my stomach, gently running her fingertips along my legs. One night she crept into bed with me as usual after the last customer had left and the girls had gone to bed. I lay on my side in a delicious half-waking state. I felt her ripe breasts squeezed against my back, her large taut nipples pressing into my flesh. She nibbled my ear-lobe. I felt her warm breath on my neck as her lips searched for mine. The tip of her moist tongue penetrated my mouth. As she rubbed the tips of my breasts with her open hands I felt wonderfully relaxed, trusting and grateful. I let myself go. Noi's hand played on the skin of my inner thighs, and I then felt her fingertips brushing up my pubic hair. My mound rose and opened with a molten gush. Noi's middle finger danced like a dervish around my clitoris, taking me to dizzy heights of sensation.

★

I lived with the other girls as if I were one of their kind. I took part in their discussions as if my concerns were the same as theirs. Whenever Doi had her painful periods, I suffered too. When Eo's baby was sick, I worried with her. When Tip got depressed, I felt down too. When Nid did her impersonations of drunken customers I laughed with the same sense of release as the others. When a customer got rough, I joined in with the girls as they came down on him like a swarm of mosquitoes and taught him a lesson. But I differed from them in one very important respect. I did not sit in the contact room or the bar. When I did go in to these places I did not stay long, as I would be taking food to the girls or carrying out other errands.

Noi did all she could to stop me from becoming a prostitute. She herself had worked and saved hard to become a *mama-san*, and did not sell her body any more, though she did sometimes have to look after influential clients who would only consider working on "management level". But this was not in the usual course of Noi's duties. She was pleased that she no longer had to put up with the drunken stares of the customers, or with their sweaty hands on her body. She wanted me to be part of the purity she had won back. In fact, although she ran a brothel Noi was sometimes like a shaven-headed Buddhist nun in a white robe. It was very touching. Later on I was to spend a lot of time thinking about all the contradictions in the concept of woman as saint and whore, but at this particular time I was not aware of these things, even though they were an important part of my life.

I was the prize on offer in a contest between Noi and Nid. Nid was one of the "shady ladies", and had moved as far away as possible from the behaviour expected of women brought up in the Buddhist tradition. She was capricious, noisy and provocative. She was unashamedly seductive towards men, and not just the customers, wore sexier clothes than the other girls and moved voluptuously. She also earned more than anyone else. She made no bones about attracting the attention of customers. Her black leather skirt was so short that it did not cover her buttocks completely, especially when her hips were in motion. This meant that she was by far the most successful at pulling the men in the contact room. But she was also the quickest worker. She took the initiative with her clients, flattering the men, admiring their erections and working so skilfully on them that often they did not even get as far as entering her. She would then take a hot towel, clean herself carefully and go back down to the contact room. She always seemed to be in a hurry, as if driven by some restless inner force.

She had a strong personality and a gift for theatre. Our favourite entertainment was watching her act out scenes between prostitute and client. She could create a dialogue between the two by playing both roles, expressing them in completely distinct movements, gestures and voices. One moment she would be the client, clumsily trying to describe his fantasies and requirements in a hoarse voice; the next she would be the tough whore, twirling a symbolic stick of sugar cane which she would then crunch between her teeth. We would be bursting with laughter, covering our mouths with our hands. These little sketches brought the girls a great sense of relief. The tears of laughter thawed the coldness in their hearts, and produced a very relaxed and loving atmosphere.

Nid began to have more and more influence over me, slowly changing both my outer and inner self. She was leading me by the hand, taking me towards a goal which deep down I already knew to be inevitable. She had an enormous supply of sexy clothes, not just the usual tart's gear. They were the tools of her trade, like her looks and her technique. The first thing she gave me was a pair of bikini-briefs, and she commented on the way they made the curves of my stomach and bottom more noticeable. Then she put me in some patent leather boots, whose heels were so high that I felt dizzy. Nid had started a nervous eating habit, so a lot of her clothes were getting too tight for her, and this meant that I assembled a basic supply of black silk underwear and nappa leather garments – revealing bras, backless tops, fishnet stockings, jump-suits and skirts. Only when it came to make-up did I show any resistance. Even later in my career all I ever used was lip-gloss. I found false eyelashes uncomfortable; they felt like some sort of foreign body which made my eyelids flutter.

Nid was so keen to transform my appearance that I got the impression she was trying to make me into what she herself would have liked to be. She helped me dress, made me move like a dancer and pose seductively. She overwhelmed me with flattery, which began to have an effect on my reaction to the surprised looks of the customers who saw me during my brief visits to the contact room. Until then I had been only vaguely aware of the effect my body could have, but now Nid had made me conscious of it. I would learn to use my body in the fight for survival.

The typhoon had blown away the cocoon. Now the moth could begin to spread its wings.

*

Noi had gone away for a few days. She wanted me to join her, but I had refused, explaining how I had to stay and help out as usual.

The night before Noi came back, Nid talked me into putting on particularly sexy clothes. I wore nothing but black, from my boots to my velvet choker. I looked in the mirror, and saw how attractive I looked. Before, I had been embarrassed to use Lek's eyes to see my reflection.

Now Nid wanted to take me to the contact room. Surprisingly perhaps, I showed no resistance, but I was suddenly overcome with stagefright. My face burned and felt as if it would explode. I even lost my sense of balance, and had to move very carefully. Nid led me there. Since it was payday the place was busy. Suddenly everyone's attention was turned on me. The girls left their clients to run up and drag me to the centre of the room. They took hold of me, turning me round and having a look at me. Customers were asked for their opinion. They began to bid for me, and the mood of excitement sent the price shooting. The girls fanned the customers' enthusiasm with no apparent regard for their own interests. They knew that I was due to become one of them, that I was to share their fate. They were like witches welcoming me to the coven at the Sabbath. Now there was no way out. All I could hope for was to find new power in this pact with darkness. I had been afraid of it before; now it was time to use the power of female sexuality to my own ends.

I felt inside that I had been initiated as a whore, even though nobody had so much as touched me between the legs. I came back down to earth, and even felt some sense of tranquility. I shooed them all off me and left the room. I could not go any further against Noi's will. I could see that she did not like the way her chick was turning into a fledgling. She knew that I was growing away from her, that I was no longer prepared to live in her warm and sheltered little fantasy world. I was very grateful to her, but I needed to be independent of her affection and money. I wanted to earn my own living and allow my brothers and sisters to lead the steady and peaceful life of rice-farmers. And, since I was a woman with only a basic education there was only one way I could achieve all this. Otherwise, I would be forced to live from hand-to-mouth, and still not be certain of being in charge of my own body, since fathers and sons of a household have exactly the same thoughts as the proprietors of restaurants and foremen on plantations and in factories. Prostitution seemed to offer me the best prospects, and I was full of youthful defiance, determined to keep damage to my body and spirit to a minimum. This was what I wanted to do, although I had no real conception of what difficulties could lie ahead.

I began to plan the practicalities of my future. Nid spurred me on in this too. I could tell that she was planning to make a move. For some time she had been working weekends in the *kosa* hotel, and this did not bother Noi, since it meant that on those days at least the other girls had a chance to earn more money. Nid had taken me with her to the *kosa* hotel once and shown me the bowling alley, the steam bath, the huge dance hall and the tiny swimming pool behind the steam bath. No-one was swimming there, though, since it was considered to be a breeding-ground for gonorrhoea.

At the weekend these were the places where men came from other areas to get together with girls, both the regulars and reinforcements from Bangkok, who would climb sleepily out of their air-conditioned bus on a Friday evening and return to the capital on Sunday. Normally, the hotel was not too busy, but at the end of the week it would liven up. Big American-style military limousines would roll up, their olive-green paintwork covered in a layer of reddish dust. This meant that they had come from distant military posts, the border controls and the anti-guerilla forces in the bush. Officers wearing beige uniforms and holsters with heavy handguns got out of these limousines. Not long afterwards the contact room at the steam bath was completely empty. The military heroes, usually well tanked-up already, would pay sixty baht an hour for the use of a hotel room, where they would be soaped up, showered and massaged. Additional services as required would hardly ever result in a tip for the girl. Other customers hired the girls for a whole night. First of all they would take them bowling, and the women would be expected to smile prettily while the men went through their drunken ritual of loud toasts to friendship and attempts at bowling. Whores depend on this kind of exclusively-masculine behaviour for their living. They also need to be protected from it.

The more senior officers put some sort of store by gallant behaviour – at least at the beginning of the evening. They sat at tables in the dimly-lit dance hall, where over-enthusiastic waiters plied them with drink. The pocket torches carried by the waiters, the stage lights and the brilliantly illuminated "birdcage" on the way to the lavatories were surrounded by gloom. The chorus-girls were provocatively dressed, with leather boots halfway up their thighs and only a hand's breadth of flesh showing below their skirts. Shrouds of smoke writhed about in the beams of light on stage and the amplified voices echoed around.

I took all this in. This, not the contact room of a provincial brothel, was to be my world. Of course, the garishly lit "birdcage" depressed me: it was right in front of the lavatories, and the girls sat in it, completely indifferent to the customers until a light was flashed into their face by the man who had chosen his dancing partner from among them. Yet I sensed that in all this there was the possibility of an escape to something better.

But Nid made sure that my ambitions did not stop there. She saw the *kosa* hotel as a dead end. As we were sipping our rice soup together one morning she said darkly:

"All we are threshing is straw. Our cut of the money is just enough for clothes and a few sweets. Where is that going to get us? In five years I'll be fat and old, plastering my wrinkles with make-up and using what little I earn to pay the quack to cure my ladies' trouble. There are just too many of us, and the competition's too tough. The Thai men are all stingy. And they're rough and inconsiderate. I wish I was a cow water buffalo! Then I'd only have to work five hours a day. The rest of the time I'd lie in the pond or the river and cool myself off. No, Malee, this can't go on. Come with me to Udon. There are *farang* men there, lots of GI's. Americans have more money and are more generous. Perhaps one of them will fall in love with you and you won't have to go on the game any more. What if he married you! Then you wouldn't have a care in the world. You could build a nice new house for your family, buy a water buffalo, and even a few *rai* of paddy fields. Come with me. You're pretty. You'll do even better than me . . . I'm off tomorrow. I'm getting up before it's light and taking the first bus. Are you coming too?"

I stared into my soup bowl. The swollen grains of rice seemed to get even bigger, ready to burst . . .

Noi would miss me. I hoped the girls would miss me as much as I'd miss them.

My answer was short. "Get me up!"

Sex Fantasyland

A whore for the Americans

A tap on the collarbone woke me with a start. Nid's hand searched for mine in the dark, and I felt her put a damp cloth between my sleepy fingers. I quickly cleaned my eyes, nose, ears, neck, armpits and feet, then I slipped on a blouse and jeans. Nid was bent over the handle of her trunk, which she had packed with our possessions the night before and then pulled quietly to the door. I darted into Noi's room and sadly laid a letter on the right-hand side of her bed. As I came out again Eo's baby was whimpering in his sleep, as if he were having a bad dream. I went and put his dummy in his mouth. He slurped at it contentedly, but then Nid hissed at me like a snake, and I hurried over to the trunk. The red light on the stairs was so dim that I almost lost my footing as I had once before.

We finally made it outside. Nothing seemed to be stirring in the dim light of early morning, but as our eyes adjusted we caught sight of the lonely *samlo* drivers flitting about like dragonflies as they searched for customers, stopping to look around while their tricycles began to roll backwards. We hailed two *samlos*, one for us and one for our heavy trunk. The two young drivers were grateful for business so early in the

33

morning and even found enough breath to laugh and chat as they pedalled along, setting to work with their wiry bodies, sinewy peasants' legs and calloused feet. When we got to the bus station the first service to Nongkhai via Udon Thani was ready and waiting. After the trunk had been loaded onto the roof Nid and I sat down on one of the narrow bus seats and huddled together for warmth. Nid's energy seemed to have ebbed, and her body was shaking. I took hold of her hand, and I think this gave her back some tranquility and confidence.

Much later, far away from home, I heard the dramatic phrase, "Every parting is a small death". As I sadly left Noi and the girls in Khon Kaen this saying would have seemed beautiful and moving to me. Yet, since that first radical departure from my village I also felt that every time I left somewhere I was being taken towards a new home. I was beginning to gain power and speed.

The bus finally reached the northern highway as day was beginning to break. I noticed for the first time the sleepy faces of all the other people who had got on. My feelings of departure, transition and hope were reflected in the glow of dawn. Yet blending with my excitement was an indulgent sense of self-pity. Here I was, so young and gentle, uprooted by forces beyond my control and forced into such a brutal profession . . . But then I suddenly felt alienated from this feeling, and was filled with new energy. That was how it had to be. The snake has to shed its skin to let its scales shine with fresh beauty.

★

As the sun rose in the sky the nervous young driver began to handle the vehicle more and more mischievously. Beneath the homemade coachwork was a Japanese Isuzu chassis, and from it came slipping, grinding, screeching and crushing noises as the gearbox responded to the driver's temperamental handling of the accelerator, clutch and gear lever. He sat half out of his seat, his body twisted to the left. In his left hand was a scrap of cloth which he used to grip at the steering wheel, but the material seemed so saturated with sweat from his hand and forehead that it did not seem to be fulfilling its purpose any more – quite the opposite! Between the thumb and forefinger of his right hand was a cigarette which he puffed at every now and then, briefly but deeply. The rear left-hand corner of the bus was open, and there stood the conductor. He was hardly more than a boy and was hanging out of the vehicle, swinging playfully in the wind, as if he were the tail of some strange bird.

Buses running the same route in Thailand are in great competition, and they are always trying to overtake each other. In this non-stop contest of speed the drivers often take very great risks, and fatal accidents are not uncommon. If you are lucky all you get is a churned-up stomach and severely strained nerves. I tried to calm myself down by watching the wide expanses of the Isan, the bushes and termite hills dotted about the fields that used to be my home.

Nid and I were pressed close against each other. Our sweat had soaked through our clothes and was mingling, making our two bodies into one.

"We must get there soon," she said, as if waking from a dream. As we shot down a hill a huge steel tower became visible, like a distant castle in the air. "The American *farang* intelligence station," commented a soldier on the other side of the gangway, before we even had the chance to ask him. "They can pick up China and Hanoi from there." Our bodies sagged with relief. The conductor called out the next stop. As we got up, the other passengers looked at us. My face began to burn. A new phrase flashed through my head: "A whore for the Americans". The trip through my homeland had suddenly

35

brought me to a strange new world. Anger and defiance rose up in me.

"Come on!" I called to Nid. "We're here."

In front of us stood the oppressive mass of the technical installation, overshadowing the other buildings straggling along the highway. The driver braked especially violently and drew up in a cloud of dust. The conductor just pushed down our trunk from the roof. It fell with such force that we could not possibly have caught it. One corner of it hit the ground, it caved in and the top flew open. Out spilled sexy underwear. Our audience burst into laughter. Another part of the old me died, and anger spurred my movements. We stuffed the lingerie back in the old tin trunk as the bus rattled into life and set off in another cloud of dust.

★

When I saw the film *High Noon* two years later at a matinee I was taken back abruptly to that morning.

In a peasant village shortly before midday we would have seen men, women and children driving water buffalo back from the fields to rest in the pool. There would have been a sense of release in the movements of man and beast as they returned from the hardest labour of the day. But here we were, standing in the blistering heat, faced with a row of locked buildings which seemed to want to shun the daylight.

There were mangy dogs lying around in the shade of the dustbins, their ribs heaving from the heat. They did the work of vultures, and had already searched for loot in the overflowing bins.

Then we saw a woman approaching from the far end of the row of buildings. Surrounding her was the heat haze, shimmering like a neon tube. We were so excited to see her that she may as well have been a supernatural apparition. We hoped

she would open the way to the world behind the closed
facades, into this dead realm guarded by predatory dogs,
which seemed to be trying to fend us off with strange symbols. Only later would we come to understand the words on
the signboards which dominated each building. They were the
names of American centres of showbusiness and entertainment. They were made more enticing with the aid of simpli-
fied sexual symbols, mostly parted legs and pouting lips.
These neon signs may have done their work at night, assault-
ing senses already bewildered by alcohol, but in the crushing
heat of midday they were guano islands in a sea of tawdry
fantasies.

When the woman finally got to us, she brought a breath of
simple, everyday reality. About twenty metres away, she
stopped to open a sliding grille in front of one of the buildings.
After she had pushed the folding metal gates sharply to either
side, she did the same to the wooden shutters behind, revealing a general store crammed with trinkets and necessities. The
sound of the doors acted as a signal, since girls now began to
emerge. They looked sleepy. Their hair was sloppily put up,
their powdered faces glowed white in the sun, and their eyes
blinked as they tried to get used to the light. They shuffled
along, their limbs still heavy with sleep.

They went to the shop, and mostly bought little things to
eat, perhaps a glass of soya milk too. And maybe a toothbrush
to replace one that had been lost. The girls did not have much
to say to each other. They seemed sullen, irritable, hung-over.

This was the world I knew so well already, and I smiled to
think how the punters would feel if they knew that their
temptresses of the night were just like everyone else. They
would probably go back remorsefully to the apron-strings of
their sweet curly-headed girls in their little home town.

"Let's have a drink," said Nid, her voice rough and hoarse,
"otherwise we'll end up like dried fruit."

We went into the shop and greeted the shopkeeper courteously. Two glasses of iced sugar-cane juice drove the sweat

from our pores, cooling us by a process of evaporation, and refreshing our stomachs.

"You're new here," said the shopkeeper, in a statement rather than a question.

"*Tschai*, we only arrived today," we answered.

This did not seem to interest most of the other girls very much, and they just shot a quick glance at us through narrowed eyes. The prospect of new competition did not seem to worry them. Only one of the girls turned to us. Her big bones, wide hips, and full bosom would have made her ideal for the task of producing a whole dynasty of peasants.

"Two more Minnie Mouses for Disneyland!" she said. "Another pair of snails with shiny lips down below, all set to raise the American flagpole. You've made it into the tarts' temple, like obedient sisters of lust. Your selfless life in this remote nunnery will bring you to the American nirvana . . ." Her loud tones broke into a cackle, and died away in sobs.

We stood like two rabbits which have been stunned with a blow to the back of the neck. The shopkeeper took pity on us.

"Don't worry," she said, "and don't be cross with her. Two days ago her regular American, her *tirak-boyfriend* was transferred home. He'd promised to take her with him, but he disappeared off without even saying goodbye. She waited for him the night before last in the bar. She was worried when he didn't turn up, and she was finally told the truth by a drunk GI who thought he had the next tenant for her basement."

This story seemed to bother Nid more than it did me. Her new illusions were being challenged. But that was the way of things, and she soon pulled herself together. "Where can we get work around here?" she asked the shopkeeper.

"In the bar?"

"Where else?"

"Well," replied the woman. "I could do with some help."

"I can guess," laughed Nid. "Fifteen baht for a twelve-hour day, no day off, and no health insurance. Too little to live on, too much to die on. And if some poor sucker knocks you up, you don't get much in the way of work and you've got three times as much to worry about. How's that for prospects!"

The shopkeeper shrugged her shoulders. "It's the same everywhere. What am I supposed to do about it?" She stared in front of her for a moment, thinking as her hands absently filled paper bags with goods. "I think a couple of girls have just been thrown out of the Las Vegas Bar. Poor things had got too old and ugly, and there was nothing soft lighting and make-up could do to help. They work the end of the street now, where the blacks go. If you can do a floorshow and speak *pasa angkrit*, then there won't be any problem, especially for the young one." She pointed to me. "You both speak English, then?"

Nid replied without a moment's hesitation. "Yes!" she said – in English. I was amazed, not knowing whether to be impressed or frightened.

"You'd do best to wait until the madame of the Las Vegas Bar comes in. She won't be long. She always drinks her iced *yakhut* here."

We dragged our heavy trunk up against the wall of the grocer's, and sat down on it, having first covered the hot metal surface with a *patung*. The sun had long passed its peak, and the day's business began to get going. The garbage men arrived, roaring like a commando troop on the attack, and threw the rubbish onto the truck as if it were hot goods. They were gone again in no time. The girls who staffed the kitchens of the bars carried baskets through the backyards to the places where they did the cooking. The doors of the bars were thrown open to let the mild afternoon breeze penetrate to their air-conditioned bowels and take the place of the cold night-time air, stale with the smell of bodies, cigarettes and alcohol. It was the only point of contact between night and day. Soon the doors would be shut again and the air-conditioning units, guardians of the passage from light to darkness, would begin to hum again. But there was still time now for the girls to meet up.

Their tempers had improved by this stage of the afternoon, and they gathered in shady spots in front of the bars, changing the place into a promenade where they gossiped, joked and teased. Business was not forgotten, though. Professional partnerships were struck up here, and warnings about bad customers exchanged. Names and descriptions were given of punters who, although they paid the bar the fee for taking a girl away before closing time, refused the next morning to give the girl the normal minimum payment of two hundred baht plus taxi or *samlo* fare which was to be expected for a little sympathy or less demanding sexual services.

We were especially interested in the talk about customers' special sexual requirements – and the payment that could be expected for satisfying them. I was amazed by what I heard, and my nervousness increased. Noi's brothel had only served Thai customers who, although often coarse and drunk, where only interested in standard vaginal sex. Special demands were rare, perhaps because these would have revealed more of their secret inner desires than they would have wanted a mere whore to know. Perhaps it was also because the girl herself set some kind of moral boundaries so that she could retain some sort of self-respect, however bruised. The girl would laugh or mock when special desires were expressed. Expecting this sort of reaction, the punter would be discouraged from the start. But it seemed that in the sex Fantasyland of Udon things were quite different. Fellatio and anal intercourse were almost the order of the day, and were therefore regarded as part of the normal service and not subject to higher rates. Customers often asked to be beaten too, and if the girl was dressed in full dominatrix gear while satisfying their masochistic demands, she was paid extra. Other way-out specialities, such as "golden showers" were mentioned, but not with particular reference to any one client. These were not part of the normal service, and assumed discretion on the part of both the client and the girl. Some needed considerable preparation – for a golden shower, for instance, the girl has to drink litres and litres of water beforehand – and since the girls were taken into the customer's confidence, they were paid much more than usual. In spite of the professional rapport between the girls they would never reveal the supplement paid; it was a trade secret. At first, I wondered whether this rule of discretion applied to customers who wanted to be degraded by beating, but I later learned that it was too common a sexual preference for the code to apply. And, once I felt at ease in this American Eldorado of sex, I got to know many of the punters through direct contact, observation and reports, and it seemed to me that this desire for degradation was simply the reverse side of the display of masculine bravado that soldiers make, especially in bars.

But I must not get ahead of myself, even though as I tell my story, I am tempted to apply later knowledge to my early inexperience.

The *mama-san* of the Las Vegas Bar came later than usual to drink her spiced and sweetened sour milk. As the sun got lower in the sky our impatience became more intense, especially Nid's, since she was reluctant to waste any time she could be using to further her new ambitions. When the shopkeeper told us that the *mama-san* was coming, Nid jumped from her seat. I restrained her by gripping her wrist: it would not have done to appear in too much of a rush. The *mama-san* spoke the Bangkok dialect with the harsh accent of the immigrant southern Chinese. She was not unfriendly, but like most Chinese businesswomen her voice was monotonously loud and assertive.

"I hear you speak English," she said, and turning to me added, "I wonder where someone as young as you could have learned it."

"I'm sorry for the misunderstanding," I answered with embarrassment. "It's true that my friend speaks English, but I only know a few words." She seemed to like my honesty, and looked at me with a pleased expression.

"Your body is as supple as young bamboo. Perhaps you'd be good in the show. You wouldn't need to speak much English to start with. And the business jargon doesn't take long to learn. And if your friend is as crafty and experienced as she seems, then she can be put to work straight away, even though I don't know anything about her. I'll give the two of you a try. Board and lodging are free. You must know the percentage rates for drinks, massage and gratification. Here we go, then."

With a great sense of relief we followed her, dragging our battered trunk behind us. Nid tugged it with particular energy: the madame's assertive style matched her own impatience. Soon we had been introduced to the other girls, had fixed up a place to sleep, and had been shown where everything was. The girls were curious about us, gently condescending about our lack of experience with the *farang*, and more than a little concerned that I was so young.

Nid flitted like a restless butterfly from one girl to another, asking endless questions and trying to learn far too many words at one go of the pidgin language the girls called English.

The *mama-san* came along after sunset and asked Nid whether she wanted to make any pick-ups that evening. Nid nodded enthusiastically, and the madame responded with irony:

"Well then, we'll push you as an innocent little country girl. Let's see if they take the bait." Everyone laughed, and Nid must have been a little ashamed at seeming so enthusiastic. Then the *mama-san* turned to me.

"I hope you're not quite so impatient, my shy little flower. I'd like to use you for the show. At the moment the only one who does a really hot number is Pim. The others move so stiffly, and look so embarrassed. It makes the Yanks feel guilty and they hide behind their last glass of beer. But you seem to have fire and venom in your body. There's poppy sap in your veins, and we need another real attraction. It'd be great to have a dancing goddess coming out from the dark, driving them wild with desire. I think you've got it in you . . . We've got enough pathetic little peasant girls who are homesick and curse having to be here, and who pray every night to Buddha for forgiveness when there's a dead-drunk GI snoring next to them. And because they can't make sense of it all they end up by getting hysterical or turning into shameless bitches. Pim will show you how to do it. Watch her dance, and learn from the mistakes of the others. Try to get into the *farang* music, don't be scared of how aggressive it is. Watch and learn. Spin your way into it like a silk-moth's cocoon. And don't get too close to the men – maybe one little look out of the corner of your eye. You must be unapproachable, our child-woman. You mustn't be some real female who can be had for two or three hundred baht a night. If you're good, I'll pay you extra, so no damage will be done to you. And any man who really wants you must be discreet, considerate and very generous. Because you're going to be our queen of the night."

My head was spinning with new thoughts and sensations. Why should a sensible Chinese businesswoman running a big bar, with over sixty girls working for her, have such high expectations of me? Of course I had some kind of idea of my looks and appeal, but there must have been more to it than that. Perhaps she could see that, in spite of my youth and my commonplace origins, I was determined to become something different from the other girls, who seemed to provoke bitterness and even disdain in her. It was with a terrible sense of astonishment that I realised she had mapped out part of the future which I myself had understood only dimly.

★

In the time that followed I was trying to find my feet in shifting sand, as new and confusing impressions made their impact on me. My lack of knowhow in the business was made clear to me on my first night in the Las Vegas Bar.

The madame had shown me a dark corner between the counter of the bar and the stage which was closed off from the audience. Once the lights had gone out I sat here out of view. The large air-conditioning unit sent blasts of cold air over my body, which was already covered in excited goose-flesh. My eyes widened with expectation as they adjusted to the intimate dimness of the lighting. The musicians struck a few notes on their electric guitars and adjusted the loudspeakers to prevent some painful feedback on the drums. The girls had put on their make-up in the washroom of the wooden lean-to which housed the lavatories, and they came from the neon-lit warmth outside to the dim darkness inside. The coloured glass dancefloor, which was lit from underneath displayed diagonal flashes every now and then. The barmen, whose white jackets gave off a bluish glow, were polishing glasses, filling the coldboxes and throwing quips at the girls, who answered back suggestively or jokingly. The barmen were diffident and polite towards me, as if the madame had given them instructions.

The musicians now began to play and sing a restrained Thai melody to warm up their voices and fingers. The main door opened for the first time that evening and the silhouette of a big man appeared in the glow of the neon lights in the street. Other figures came through the door. Three heavy men with big haunches, crew cuts, their arms and hands covered in hair and tattoos sat down at the bar. They were the first real live Americans I had ever seen. My body suddenly felt very fragile. I looked at the other girls. Many of them were gracefully formed, and I dreaded to think of those great buffalos of men forcing their way between those narrow hips. The mere thought of it gave me a pain in the groin.

An advance party broke off from the groups of girls around

the room. Four or five of them left the others talking around them and made their way towards the Americans. I noticed that they were some of the taller and more sturdily built of my new colleagues. Either they must have had these visitors as previous customers, or they were not bothered by the thought of heavy physical acts with these giants. This sort of choice was made consciously by the girls and it represented some sort of vital personal freedom left to them, although it may have been, of course, that financial necessity forced their decision. It was really the pathetic remains of the union of chosen lovers, but it was also the manifestation of a secret hope, however tortured, of liberation from this life of prostitution through the existence of a faithful partner. I later learned that these very moral and conventional desires on the part of the girls led time and again to romances with foreigners which carried all their hopes – and which led to ever deeper scars. But these desperate hopes leading to the risks of another romance were exactly what made Asiatic Suzie Wongs like me so desirable to the Americans. Much later, when I began to work St. Pauli in Hamburg, I found a quite different attitude among the prostitutes. There, most of the girls found themselves caught up in a petit-bourgeois mentality, despising the "immoral" punters, and quite unaware that their pimps were a substitute for a respectable husband. It was all routine to them, and they had about as much enthusiasm for their job as workers on the early shift in a factory.

In the Las Vegas Bar the customers were quite free to approach the girls, but it would not be a good idea for a man to express a preference for a girl who had made no advances to him. Inexperienced punters often did not wait for this signal, propositioned the girl quite unexpectedly, mistook Siamese restraint for tacit agreement, and forced the girl's choice by then paying the madame to release her for the evening. The girl's revenge varied from trick to trick, but the punter was unlikely to enjoy much of an erotic experience, and usually had to pay over the odds. Once he was ready for action and

45

attempting entry, the girl, if she was slight in build, would begin to complain about how much it hurt, and it would have needed a hardened sadist not to take any notice. Either that, or she talked about her baby, and her lover far away, also a GI, who was back home saving for her to go over and join him. What American soldier would not be shamed into stopping there and then? There are lots of ways to deflate a man . . .

When the girls approached the Americans at the bar, they used one of two methods. The differences between these were representative of the contradictions and cultural schizophrenia of this sexual funfair. Some of the girls were hesitant, glancing furtively, fluttering their eyelids, acting, in fact, according to the Thai code of behaviour. Other girls were loud-mouthed and unashamed, trying to imitate what they thought to be American behaviour. They paraded past the men, tweaked them and tittered "Darling".

It was interesting to see which methods of seduction were successful. I certainly did not want to be that shameless in my behaviour. I thought there was more potential in being distant, but enticing, so indicating that I was more expensive to come by.

In the meantime three of the girls had made it to become the front runners. They were now sitting with their heavyweight Romeos on a corner seat and drinking whisky and coke to liven things up. The men had insisted on tasting the drink to check that there really was whisky in there. It was not enough for them just to obtain the girl's bodies, which they were now pawing possessively, they also wanted to influence their mental state and their self-control, and did not like the girls to remain sober as they got drunker and drunker in front of them. This meant that many of the girls ended up with terrible inflammations of the stomach. What is more, drink had become a necessity for many of them as they tried to get over their sense of aversion, disgust and self-contempt.

The first deals had been made. It was only nine o'clock

when the three couples left the bar, the men having paid comparatively high release fees for the girls, who were really meant to remain on duty till one o'clock.

The bar was now packed with customers. The barmen performed their various duties with a seamless professionalism born of long experience. The waiters were benign genies who were always there when needed. They served a kind of food I had never seen: huge chunks of grilled meat with a T-bone through them, which came with bright green peas and strips of potato; piled-up triangles of bread with stuff inbetween them; and big, soft, slimy things which, although piled high with other items, were not very solid, and were soon reduced from a great edifice to a shapeless mess. These were known as hamburgers. After eating these you had to lick your fingers. This way of eating seemed quite barbaric to me, and I could never get completely used to it.

I was particularly fascinated by the American language. I was going to have to be able to find my way around in it, and quite apart from not being able to understand it, it seemed strange to me in other ways – oddly inarticulate, deliberately sloppy. And it was very loud, something that could be attributed both to the larger vocal chords of the foreigners and their own way of speaking. I may have been just a simple peasant girl, but my parents and the teacher at the temple school in our village had put great store by a traditional Siamese upbringing, which meant, among other things, speaking with restraint when in public or with strangers, quietly and *supab* – with conscious courtesy. The gentleness of a girl's voice was supposed to be charming. What a contrast to the loud confusion of words around me, with roaring male voices and the strained shrillness of the girls trying to keep up with them. It was all an insult to my trained ears.

But the sex playground had also developed its own language, a pidgin which made communication easier. Both sides adapted to it, and the Las Vegas Bar ended up being called the

Lat Viga Bar by the customers as well as the staff. Thais cannot pronounce the final "s" in everyday speech and tend to make it into a "t", whereas in pidgin it is often completely passed over. In fact, pidgin can work in an extraordinary way. For instance, words like *mama-san* (madame) and *baby-san* (baby) date from the time of the American occupation of Japan, and words with the Japanese suffix *san* have been fully adopted in the pidgin Thai of the girls in the bars. "You make sweet eyes" means "You're a flirt", and "You butterfly" means "You're unfaithful". Even the raw side of the business has become translated into metaphors, like "smoke cigar" for fellatio. Later, when I went to Pattaya, I discovered the German influence on the prostitutes' pidgin language, for example using *bum-sing* (from the German *bumsen:* meaning to screw or to fuck).

When I first arrived in Udon I suffered from real culture shock, even though the girls had warned me about it. The *farangs* often behaved in a way which went against so many of our traditions. We make a respectful greeting with the *wai*, in which we put the palms of our hands together and raise them; the American forms of greeting seemed incredible to me, from the curt "Hi!", through the vice-like grip of the hand-shake, and to the "hearty" slap on the back – which is enough to break your spine! I was particularly shocked by the unrestrained use of swearing, even in compound words. I was later interested to see that while the Germans swear with an anal orientation, the Americans tend to refer to the genitals. But it was the scornful arrogance of these foreigners and their lack of sensitivity that I found the most objectionable. Only a small number of them allowed the Thais to keep a sense of self-respect. The Americans, with their technological culture, and its sober, functional logic, must have lost any ability to empathise with other ways of thinking. I was often to hear Americans complaining of Thais who, when asked the way somewhere, had pointed them in the wrong direction. I can just imagine the situation. An American goes up to a Thai and says, "Hey, buddy, know the way to the Mithrapap Highway?" The Thai does not know the way, but he does not want to lose face and ends up guessing. The American ends up in the jungle cursing the Thais for their stupidity. If, however, he had asked the way by saying, "I would be interested to know if anybody could possibly answer my difficult question as to how I can get to the *Tanon Mithrapap* from here," the Thai would have done his utmost to help, since he would have stood to gain respect.

The girls had to become completely indifferent to their old patterns of behaviour, otherwise life in this isolated "Fantasyland" caused considerable psychological stress. All the Thais in this cut-off place had got used to the way Americans kiss in public, hold a girl's head, or sit with their feet up in someone else's direction – all of which are taboo to us. Outside the ghetto much *farang* behaviour was acutely embarrassing to the girls. Moreover, they must have felt stigmatised both by the "upper echelons" of Thai society, who branded them as immoral and unpatriotic, while the ordinary working folk often bitterly reproached them for taking advantage of prostitution as their sole opportunity of escaping the "confederacy of the poor". As a result the foreigners' whores were frequently the victims of jibes and insults from Thai youths who saw them as outcasts yet begrudged them for being beyond their price range. It was not surprising, then, that the girls moved in a particular milieu of bars, restaurants, hairdressing salons, shops, cinemas and modes of transport, most of whose business relied on them. Any lover who wanted to get a girl out of this world with no trouble was really taking on quite a task.

★

On my first evening in the Las Vegas Bar I concentrated mainly on the stage, which I was watching from one side. The show ran non-stop from seven o'clock onwards, although it was fairly monotonous most of the time. According to how many girls were needed on bar duty, there were one, two, three or four go-go girls on the stage, moving to the rhythm of the background music. I was to discover that most of these girls were among those who were most aggressive and uninhibited at the bar. There were also young and pretty girls displaying themselves on the stage, but the most violent and thrustingly suggestive movements in time to the heavy rhythms were made by girls who were older and wanted to use the stage to make themselves more sought-after and expensive. This meant that when there was not much business to be had the madame had to prevent a rush for the stage, and the unoccupied girls ended up dancing in couples on the floor.

More or less every half hour the band announced an important number with a few tremolos, red spotlights began to scour the stage, the music became quieter and more seductive, and one of the dancing-girls came out of the darkness and began a striptease. I soon noticed that four of the girls performed in a drearily similar manner. They all used the same sort of tawdry gear like peacock feathers, feather boas and chiffon. Their strip followed the same rituals, often not even in time with the music, and with a painfully bland expression on their faces. The last, in fact the only, surprise before the lights went out was the state of the dancer's bodies – wrinkles, sagging bottoms and pendulous breasts. I felt sorry for these women, who attracted more whistles than applause and had to put up with catcalls during their performance. The Las Vegas Show would have been a very sad affair if Pim had not taken the stage.

Pim was an experience. She was like a whirlwind, flirtatious, narcissistic and exhibitionistic, full of life and excitement as she performed. She dressed differently from the other strippers. She wore a skintight leotard, which she never took off completely, even at the climax of the dance. Only occasionally did she caressingly expose one small, firm breast with its round, hard nipple and almost total lack of aureola. Her bottom was round and firm, with a touch of childish softness about it, and it was this part of her anatomy which formed the centre of her erotic magic show and conveyed the sexual message. And this anal come-on worked. Every time Pim danced the spectators got hot under the collar. They always called wildly for encores, but Pim did not come back. The band just suggested that she was coming on again later, and so kept a large proportion of the customers in the bar, raring for more.

As the evening wore on I was amazed at how involved I got in the show. I hated the way the four girls did such a bad striptease, and felt stirrings of ambition when Pim pulled off another successful performance. Hundreds of ideas ran through my head. I would discuss them with the madame. I had to become a professional as soon as possible, since I had got myself into this business and wanted to make a success of it. A wild spirit took hold of me. Sex and danger, sex and death, sex and power, sex and survival. These dark, voracious feelings, part of the whore's practical philosophy were later to find symbolic expression in a scene I witnessed at the Circus Krone, where a beautiful and voluptuous blonde in a scanty tiger-skin costume tamed huge Bengal tigers. When she put her head between the jaws of the principal animal and finally made as if to kiss him, I shuddered with excitement. Behind the bars of the cage was a heightened metaphor of my own life.

Since that first evening in the Las Vegas Bar I have often wondered whether sexual exhibitionism is a particular characteristic of prostitutes. I will not try to answer this complicated moral question, but will only say that from the blinkered behaviour of a frisky mare, to the wheedling of a secretary in search of a wedding ring and the identification of a sensitive actress with an erotic role, there exists a wide range of deliberately exhibitionistic behaviour.

My entry into the erotic show and into seduction was a consummate piece of theatre. And this theatricality was both a triumph of technique and the result of an increasingly deep identification with the part.

My first thought was not of the power and success that the demon sex could bring me. What I had to do right now was get the right equipment.

After the bar had closed for the night the madame called me to see her. "How did you like the show?" she asked. I answered hesitantly:

"I can learn a lot from Pim."

She laughed. "Yes, you're right there. The others are a real disaster."

"Perhaps they don't like the show, and would really rather work the bar," I said, trying to smooth the way.

Among the other girls Pim moved like a diaphanous-tailed fighting fish among common carp. I knew I had to be careful not to make her vanity turn into jealousy. The madame led me to the centre of the circle of girls, announcing that the show was to be made bigger and better. The other girls showed no signs of life, but Pim's eyes flashed with surprise. Then the madame made a crafty opening gambit:

"Pim, the new girl would like to learn from you to begin with, because she liked your dancing so much." Pim's face immediately relaxed into a smile and she took my hand, saying:

"But you're still so young!"

Then she laughed. "Never mind, I'll make you into a star of the dance halls."

I had managed to get in. Pim took me under her wing, and I

found out that she had formulated a professional method which she worked at instilling into me. I was immediately surprised by her keep-fit routine. While the other girls slept into the early afternoon, Pim was doing exercises in the nearby Turkish baths in the late morning. She had also built certain yoga exercises such as the *pflug* into her routine. With an iron will I would not have expected from her she went through it every day, even if she had been with a client the night before, which happened about twice a week. She was every expensive, and always assessed the customer carefully first.

I followed her exercise routine, not simply because I was eager to learn, but also because I soon began to be very aware of my body, which made me feel more self-confident, optimistic and at peace with myself.

Pim put her show together very conscientiously. She often talked to the musicians to find out about new fashions in music, and she rehearsed with them in detail, including the lighting. Until then I had virtually no experience of Western music. Pim explained to me the differences between pop, rock, blues and bar music, between standards, hits, and flashes in the pan. She also made clear how important it was to combine music, erotic movement and deliberate sexual messages in a harmonious whole. She formulated this blend through her perceptiveness and from several years' experience of what worked for which men.

"Whenever you go on stage, test the atmosphere, and you'll know straight away what's needed. You'll be able to sense whether most of the men there want you to run about with an elephant's tusk in your pussy, or whether you need to flash your bum at them. But whatever you do, do it with style. Leave all those basic tricks with Coke bottles to the girls who haven't got any imagination."

After a week of intensive work with Pim and then with the musicians, she was pleased with the way I had got on. It was agreed with the madame that my first appearance should be on the following Sunday. I had only rehearsed one number in detail, with *Blueberry Hill* by Fats Domino as the backing, a song which seemed to have a particularly strong combination of rhythm and easy melody. My number had no theme as yet, no gimmick. It was just going to test that I had learned the basics of erotic dance, including some acrobatics.

My first performance was due. The bar was packed on Sunday evening, and the thick wall of sound around me seemed to be one solid hum. I felt alone and rejected. As the stagelights dimmed and the band began their tense tremolo, Pim took me by the elbow and led me to the centre of the dark stage. She opened her broad, floor-length cape of glittering black material, pressed my body to hers, and covered us both up. The singer of the band announced my appearance dramatically. He called me Pim's "baby", building up to these words: "Gentlemen, tonight, beneath the spotlight, you will see an ugly little caterpillar turning into an incredibly beautiful, dancing butterfly!"

At that moment I was pressing my scantily clad body against Pim's breasts, stomach and thighs. I wanted to become one with her flesh so as to escape the stagelights. But Pim had the cruelty of a mother bird who pushes her fledglings from the nest so that they might fly. As the spotlight flashed on, she suddenly opened her arms wide and stood back from me. A growl of surprise rose from deep in the throats of the male audience. There was a sharp burst of applause, then the music began, relaxing my tense limbs. I could breathe again, and my lungs wanted to expand into infinity. I did not need to feel for the rhythm of the music, it was pulsing within me. I worked at enlivening each movement, and my limbs shuddered with energy. Once I had shown myself, I drew back from the beam of light, becoming an innocent child again, only to step forward once more, making lascivious movements. For the first time I felt the heady pleasure of exhibitionistic sensuality. I wanted my body to be admired. I was in love with myself. I arrogantly accepted the homage of throaty, moaning cries which the audience could hardly keep to themselves. I decided to experience this sense of demonic power again and again, yet at the same time I heard a quiet voice warning me against obsessiveness, reminding me of the need for modesty, since power is a transitory thing. I made an offering to this spirit in the last wild movements of my dance, ending up like a dazed bird on the floor in a meditative gesture of frailty. I stayed there until the rain of applause brought me back to reality.

The audience were whistling and stamping their feet. The band played a fanfare and Pim lifted me up and hugged me. My cheeks began to burn, and I ran backstage for refuge. I needed to sort out my feelings.

Then Nid came to me. She was very moved.

"My little one, you will go far. I am glad that you were so good."

I took her hand, happy to have her near me. At that moment, just when I needed it, she brought back thoughts of the past and dreams of the future.

"I will have some time for you now, Nid," I said. "You must tell me what has happened to you in the meantime." I was ashamed to think that I had found virtually no time for her during the intensive preparation for the show.

Later, the madame came to me, and, in her curt, businesslike way, said:

"OK, I was right about you. You'll be paid from now on, though you'll get less than Pim. Here are your wages."

She pressed eight hundred baht into my hand. I blushed with delight.

I was so excited that I slept very badly that night, but my morning exercise with Pim brought me back down to earth. We were boisterous and playful, and Pim pushed me just as I was finding my balance in a handstand. I ran after her and pulled her down, we wrestled on the ground like tussling children, and finally lay exhausted, Pim on top of me. Her lips approached mine slowly and she gave me a long, gentle kiss. I embraced her and pressed her softly to me.

She slapped me on the bottom, and told me to get dressed.

"We must be off to town!"

We went by taxi to Udon, walked into a branch of the Bank of Ayuddhaya, and Pim helped me to open my first bank account; I deposited seven hundred baht. The teller was very helpful, and I felt more optimistic than I had in a long time. We then bought pieces of salted pineapple wrapped in newspaper from a street vendor, and eventually decided to go to the cinema.

They were showing *Love Is a Many Splendoured Thing*, based on the book by the Eurasian authoress Han Suyin. The romantic story of love between East and West carried us away to a world of yearning hopes and sentiment. The romanticised love between the races in the film let us think about our work as whores to the foreigners as something more beautiful. I said we were like the *durian* fruit, fine flesh within a foul-smelling skin.

When we left the cinema the sun had already gone down. The lights were lit in the shops and on the street stalls. I dampened a handkerchief and wiped the dried salt of tears from the corner of my eyes. After one last sigh Pim had her feet back on the ground again, ready to face reality. She blew her nose, so that she could smell the tempting aromas of the hot food in the street stalls. Frying garlic made my mouth water too. We had the evening off, so we could live it up a little.

We sat down at a pleasant corner bar. There were little oil-lamps on the table, and beneath them glowed spirals of incense, which smelled of sandalwood and kept the mosquitoes away. There were three large electric fans on the ceiling, which as they turned made a rushing sound like kites flying past, bringing a stimulating and refreshing breeze. We ordered a large dish of *satay*. We dipped the little skewers of

56

meat in a sweet sauce seasoned with garlic and chilli, and grilled them over a flame in the middle of the table. Pim motioned to a waitress, and with a mischievous look at me out of the corner of her eye she ordered two bottles of soda water, a flask of *Mekhong* whisky and a dish of *manau*, sour lime. Pim darkened the soda water in my glass with whisky, then lightened it again with lime juice. It did not even occur to me to resist alcohol, which I had never drunk before, since today everything seemed so vivid, so animated and benevolent. I wanted to try everything and anything. Although I tried to drown the taste of the whisky with the lime juice, I liked the effect it produced. It was a kind spirit which rid me of all my worries and threw them away like a wet sisal sack. I put my shoulders back, the better to let the sunny warmth invade my stomach. My imagination was swelling like seed corn, and my eloquence was the earthly shadow of my soaring thoughts.

Pim, who could hold her drink much better than I, was a restrained and affectionate listener. I began to tell her at random some of the ideas that had struck me for the show at the Las Vegas Bar. She was interested by them. I tried to bring my thoughts and words together, and to speak more slowly and coherently. I noticed that Pim's eyes were becoming more fixed and closer to me. Then, my confidence fired by the drink, I sensed that the spark had caught, and that the flames were spreading. Another bottle of whisky turned the smouldering flames into a roaring blaze. We went home by taxi at some time around midnight. We were still whispering to each other about our plans as we stood before the dormitory door. Our partnership was sealed with a gentle goodnight kiss.

The next morning Pim found me at the tap swilling down water like a calf dying of thirst. She took me to the shower, found the largest ladle she could, and splashed me so hard with water that I begged her to stop. She finally threw the aluminium spoon to the ground, where it bounced and clattered.

"Do you want to drown me, you poisonous watersnake?" I panted.

Pim clenched her teeth and hissed through them at me:

"You must have a clear head today. We're starting work on the new show."

She rubbed my head. Then she took hold of a thick tress of my hair close to the roots, and, with all her might, pulled my head up. I screamed with shock and pain. Pim just laughed and dribbled hair-oil and rose-water onto my scalp and massaged it gently. As the blood began to circulate vigorously it pushed the blockage from my brain.

After our exercise session I felt wide awake once more. As we had agreed the previous evening, we met up with the madame. She sat in front of us with curlers in her hair, chewing pieces of mango. It was rather difficult under these circumstances for us to explain the erotic content of our new show. But she was a real professional, and caught on immediately. She was encouraging, and promised to support us all the way. So we set to work.

We went to Udon and asked the cinema management for the name of the painter who did the huge billboards which were put up in front of the cinema for each film. The painter proved to be a shy young man who made nervous little gestures with his hands to underline his rapid speech. He seemed so different from the garish posters he painted. We asked if he was capable of more delicate work, and his interest was immediately aroused. We then told him what we had in mind – a screen about four metres high and eighteen wide, stretched with canvas, and which could be set up to form a half-octagon. On it would be painted an idyllic country landscape. In the centre of it would be two small farms with ox-carts, water buffalo and domestic animals between them. On the left would be an elegant temple *sala*, on the right a bamboo thicket with a stream coming from it; in the background would be rice fields. The painter liked our ideas, made sketches in the air, and suggested improvements. After we had told him to get some money in advance from the madame, we left happily.

Then we went to find Arun, the bandleader. His name meant "sunrise", but that lunchtime he looked as though he had drunk too much *Sundowner* whisky the night before. We teased him about the bags under his eyes, which did nothing to improve his mood. But he was not angry, because he was really a very good friend. He was a *gatoy* and was always getting mixed up in unhappy love affairs with young men who, unlike him, were not ready to be faithful. Our light-hearted chatter soon managed to divert his thoughts and cheer him up a little. We told him about our new show, and explained that we really needed his help. He liked our ideas, and he began excitedly to dig out melodies from his memory and to hum them to us.

My basic idea for the show was really very simple. Our life was being spent on an artificial American island, in a sex Fantasyland. We were subjected defencelessly to an alien force which turned us into ridiculous Minnie Mouse figures. The present show was a childish reflection of the American concept of theatrical sexual illusion, which meant that we could never be credible and therefore never successful in selling our sexuality. What we needed was to get back on home ground. What was familiar to us was exotic to the punters. What we found reassuring, they found mysterious and enticing. By adding an erotic impact to scenes from our village life, it would be easy for us to write the scenario, but the spectators would be viewing the age-old travellers' dream of sunny and exotic islands of love.

This was why Pim and I had commissioned the large theatrical backdrop, and our idea also meant that Arun, who had once studied classical Thai music, could indulge himself in musical memories. He searched out gentle traditional melodies for us which would provide a contrast to the rock rhythms. Pim and I began to practise folk dance again, and worked at remembering the movements of classical dance.

The backdrop was ready in a week. The painter had transformed our pastoral idyll. It seemed to be viewed through a soft-focus lens, and its sweep made it look like a real landscape reaching to the horizon. He had succeeded in conjuring up the atmosphere of life on the land on the stage of the Las Vegas Bar. The width of the backdrop allowed us to perform different dances in front of different sections of scenery.

We translated scenes from peasant life into dance, and set about co-ordinating ordinary movements with the music in order to produce, almost imperceptibly, an erotic effect. The commonplace was to be rediscovered in a seductive new form.

First of all we rehearsed the harvest dance of the rice-reaping women. In this, we included the other strippers from the bar. Working as a group livened up almost all the girls, and they developed a new sense of daring and even relish for their work. Our artful revival of the past was very enjoyable. At the beginning of this particular dance each of us was covered completely with the exception of our hands and feet. We were wearing dark blue collarless peasants' shirts, and a simple wrapover skirt. Our heads were covered with a *pakomah*, leaving only a slit for the eyes. (In real life this acts as a protection from the heat and the dust, and soaks up sweat.) Each of us held a sickle. We stood in front of the right-hand section of the background, and, equipped with just these basic costumes and props, we began a dance filled with a wicked eroticism.

To begin with, our backs swayed and the sickles swung, creating an harmonious image of the age-old rhythm of reaping. Then Arun broke up the disciplined sequence of the traditional music, struck strange jazz-rock chords on his guitar, and we spread out. We carefully placed the sickles behind the neck of the person next to us, so forming a dangerously linked semi-circle. Our movements became more free, and no longer expressive of working on the land.

The sharp sickles set our nerves on end too in the dance. We untied our *patung*, exposing our stomachs and the tiny briefs we were wearing. Then we increased the titillation by slowly undoing the buttons of our blouses, finally revealing our breasts in their tiny lace bras. But our heads were still covered with the *pakomah*. We had become grotesque erotic figures, finally placing the sickle between our legs and swinging it back and forth, threatening to slit ourselves open from the crotch to the navel. This scene always made the spectators grunt with excitement. But we were not going to let the men get away with enjoying our masochistic threats! In the finale of the dance we turned the sickles round, and knelt behind a small sheaf of rice stalks, tied together just beneath the heads of grain, which made the whole sheaf look like a phallus. We then caressed the stem of the sheaf, stroked the head of grain, and finally pretended to slice the stem from the root and throw it behind us.

The girls in the bar shrieked with pleasure at the perform-ance. The men's reactions were varied. Some were driven wild by it, while others did not like it at all.

We usually followed this scene with a dance which the customers found rather more comfortable. In it, Pim and I played a loving couple. She wore the old-fashioned, diagonal-ly wound breeches of the princes of the *Ramakien*, the ancient epic of the gods. I wore the heavy golden dress of the temple dancer. A woman as a masculine seducer seems to be one of the strongest erotic cues for man. It oversteps the norm of hetero-sexuality without, perhaps, wounding delicate male pride.

In this dance Arun even used traditional percussion and wind instruments. The seduction scene took place on the left-hand side of the backdrop in front of the temple. We courted each other hesitantly with archaic gestures. Pim's movements became more and more flirtatious and fiery. She finally took hold of a short stick of bamboo which still had the bulb at its upper end. While Arun played the flute, she gently brought the bamboo to her mouth and began to caress the bulb with her lips, and enticed me to the other side of the backdrop where there was the bamboo-grove and the stream. She ran the stick of bamboo over my body, as if to rub away the shield of resistance. She then broke the spell, dared to kiss me, and entwined herself around me like a many-limbed deity. My dress fell from me to reveal a scanty white leotard. She sprinkled my breasts and crotch with water, supposedly from the stream, which made the thrusting buds of my nipples and the dark pomegranate of my genitals show through seductively. As she wrapped herself around me ever more closely and greedily, one of her breasts became exposed, to show once again how the woman-man figure desired the child-woman. The lights dimmed and the taped sound of a tropical storm thundered around as the curtains closed.

So we gradually created a new and imaginative show, which took the themes for the dances from the painted backdrop. There was only one number where it was not used in this way.

My inspiration for that particular number came from my outings with Arun. He had a big Suzuki motorbike, and he often took me on wild afternoon rides in the country. I never wore a crash helmet and always left my hair loose. The hot air rushing past pulled at the roots of my hair and my face was whipped with silky thongs, while the wind rushed into my nostrils and filled the space around my brain with soft cushions of air. My eyes devoured the ever-changing view. It was only after I had been out with him a few times that I hesitantly asked Arun if I could take over the handlebars from him. He turned off from the Mithrapap highway onto an unsurfaced side road, where he explained how to change gear. Once I had lost my initial fear of the powerful growls coming from the depths of the machine I soon learned how to restrain it, and finally dared to go beyond third gear.

My trips with Arun brought me more than simple pleasure in learning to control and harness the powerful monster beneath me. These cross-country journeys were like a witch's flight to deserted places. I drove with my engine roaring and bellowing through the countryside of my childhood and its idyllic scenes. I shouted my longing to the winds, screamed my hatred of the land that had made me an exile. I used the wild power between my legs to express my angry sorrow. My eyes crossed the countryside, the machine followed me, and I took my farewell. I was so excited by all this that the pointed tips of my breasts almost became sore from the wind resistance. This made me wish that Arun was more than just a dear gay friend. I wanted to press my haunches against a throbbing rod of masculinity, feel a searching hand move towards the ripe fruit of my vulva, there to have its gentle yet wild fingers dampened by the flow of my sweet juices.

One afternoon I asked Arun if we could capture one of these trips and make it into an erotic scene for the show. The country had made me into a whore, and I was not going to let it forget that. It too was going to become part of my prostitute's world. It was not going to remain hypocritically immune.

I asked Arun if it would be possible to film one of our trips and project this film onto a screen on the stage, to be run with a soundtrack of taped engine noise.

"That wouldn't be hard," he said, "but what's the point of it?"

I explained that I was considering a scene with me, Pim and the motorbike (which could easily be pushed on stage). Our erotic play would take place on the motorbike in front of the back projection. I wanted it to look so real that when it went over a bump the audience's stomachs would sink.

Arun laughed. "The way you drive, we'd better get sick bags ready for them!" But he set to work straight away. I borrowed a cine camera from the madame, and bought a

projector on the company. Then we went for a really wild
ride. Arun held me with one arm – I hope that did not bother
him too much – and with the other he held the camera, which
was attached to a harness on his shoulder.

When the developed film was shown to Pim, we were all
very excited about it. The landscape rushed up to us, and we
felt every bump in the road.

As far as the costumes for this number were concerned, only
black dominatrix gear would do. We had high-heeled patent
leather boots which came up to our thighs, glistening back ciré
gloves past our elbows and a one-piece costume of the same
material which exposed plenty of our darkly gleaming skin
covered in palm oil. The ultimate symbol of our power was a
whip made up of leather strips wound together. The motorbike between our thighs was the beast we would tame and
bring to submission. To add an extra sinister thrill we wore
wooden masks with distorted features, taken from traditional
story-telling dance. At the beginning of the scene it was still
dark, and we were half-lying face down on the bike. The film
showed a still of a road running to the horizon. The motor was
already ticking over and revved up as the picture began to
move. The crazy ride began. The band struck tough chords.
"Eve of destruction – The Eastern World, it is exploding . . ."
The motor was roaring, the hard rock was belting out, and
then we came up front, wild sexual furies, cracking our whips,
making way for our ride on the machine from Hell. A bike is
not much like a couch, but we managed to perform our antics
on it, moving like gravity-defying highwire artists. We wrapped ourselves around each other, engaging in combat with
violent thrusts from the groin, as if love and hatred were
indivisible. It was wild. We could not have given any more of
ourselves. We finally slipped off, lubricated by the covering of
sweat on our bodies. That was how our show ended. The
audience was roaring with applause, but we just rushed off
hand–in–hand, our flanks quivering, and in the washroom

poured ladle after ladle of water over our heads and bodies with our tired arms. It seemed as if we were trying to reduce the heat of our bodies to the temperature of the water.

★

The atmosphere in the Las Vegas Bar became noticeably better. The madame was very happy about things, as there had been such an increase in custom that a new doorman was needed, and each person was spending more money too. More customers and the hot show meant that the girls stood to make better business too, so the income from services rendered went up increasingly. It was all going really well.

My wages had gone up to twelve hundred baht a week. I was earning nearly as much as the governor of a province. He would have illegal earnings on top of that, but then I was making extra money too.

The madame had suggested that I be sparing with my favours, if I was to give them at all, that is. I had stuck to this, and was not to be had in the ordinary run of things, since I kept to the sections of the bar reserved for staff. Of course, people called to me, invited me for drinks, and made straightforward propositions via the barmen and the other girls, who were tipped for their pains.

I was forced to remember time and again my bold resolution to try and keep my body as intact as possible. I could see that this was going to be difficult. But I was perversely determined to make more out of fantasies and thrills than by putting myself up for a big turnover on the meat market.

The madame got me my first client. It was after the last number of the show. I had showered and dried myself, and was on the way to the bar for a last small bottle of beer. Then I met her.

"Are you tired?" she asked me in her direct way. "We've got a big one here. There's a man who's interested in you. He's not young, but he's generous. An important American. He likes you. He asked if you were discreet. I said yes. Is two thousand baht OK?"

That was an offer even Pim would have found impossible to refuse.

The madame gave me an address. "You don't need any special gear. I think he likes the childish, naive bit."

The taxi took me to a large house with a big garden. An elderly housemaid took me to the bedroom, which had comfortable rattan furniture and a refreshing electric fan instead of air-conditioning. I was left in there alone. Eventually the door of the adjoining bathroom was opened by a man of about fifty-five. He greeted me politely with "*Savaddhi krap*" and a rather awkward *wai*. As I courteously answered "*Savaddhi ka*" I looked surreptitiously at him. He was wearing a kimono of dark silk, and had short, bristly, dark hair streaked with grey. His face was weatherbeaten, with a deep scar over the left eyebrow. His eyes seemed to be deep in thought. His hands made me feel less anxious. They were large, powerful and hairy, but I could imagine them playing a stringed instrument with sensitivity. I spoke using the polite form of Thai:

"Sir, I am at your disposal until daybreak." He smiled, and answered in English:

"Unfortunately, I don't speak Thai. Could you tell me your name?" He liked its sound. "Malee, would you undress for me?"

He was a real sugar daddy. It pleased him that I was young, and he treated me with care, as if I were his daughter – in fact, that must have been the special thrill for him, since he sometimes mentioned his real daughter. I undressed with modest movements and folded my clothes on a side-table like a well brought-up child. Then I lay down on the freshly starched sheet covering the wide rattan bed. He sat at its foot. I gave him a little smile, eager that my services should be to his satisfaction. I wriggled like a lizard. His eyes became glazed, ever more deeply lost in desire and memories. He took hold of me gently, as if I were a precious jade carving being examined by a connoisseur. He rubbed my nipples softly between thumb and forefinger, and they sprang up automatically. Then everything happened very quickly. He threw off his kimono, I parted my thighs and felt him on top of me. He smelled of tobacco, mouthwash and bittersweet cologne. He was careful not to kiss me on the mouth. I would have hated that. He rested on his elbows so that I could breathe easily. Although I had applied plenty of lubricant cream in preparation it hurt my vagina a little as he entered, but I told him it did not. Eventually, the muscular channel relaxed and became a slippery chute with the help of the cream and drops of fluid from his erection. He stammered a pet name I did not understand. It probably was not me he was thinking about. Then his thrusting accelerated to an abrupt finish. All that could be felt was the rhythm of his ejaculation. He moaned, paused, reached for a box of Kleenex, and finally withdrew from me. We lay beside each other for a while. He thanked me. After we had showered he lit a cigarette and we sat opposite each other, there on the bed, wrapped in our towels with our legs crossed. Our eyes met mischievously, driven by a common impulse I cannot explain. We laughed, truly relaxed. There was a delightful sense of poetry I have only experienced very rarely with clients since.

"Malee, you must go now. I am an old man with my own little ways, and I need my sleep. But I would like to know if you could visit me every Friday night. On the same financial terms, of course. There isn't much room for fantasy in my life, but you bring me some."

He watched with pensive pleasure as I dressed unhurriedly. He reminded me about the envelope on the table. I smiled at him as I left, and bowed my head in a particularly respectful *wai.* I had found my first regular client – and, in a way, a friend as well.

My most persistent admirer turned out to be a guy everybody called "Captain". He was a nightmare of a man, at least to a Thai. He was taller than any of us, standing one metre ninety. Nearly every evening his huge Honda roared up to the bar in a cloud of exhaust fumes. Then he would swagger into the bar in his leathers and crash helmet. This covered his whole head, had a smoked glass visor and the words *Captain America* painted on it in fluorescent letters. Everything about him was black. I like black. It is the colour of both corruption and purity, the light of night, and the light of hope before dawn. But on him it seemed wrong, lacking in depth. What I mean is, I did not like him. It angered me to see the way his rough and aggressive behaviour forced men to their knees and twisted them into creatures belonging to his world. Nobody put up any resistance to him. And it made him mad not to have me. I always put him down by simply ignoring him. For me he was the embodiment of barbaric arrogance. I was going to make him aware of the gentle power and soft strength of Asia. His invitations became more brash and forceful. I became more unapproachable. He had already given up trying to talk to me directly, because then he would have had to suffer the secret malicious satisfaction of all the others. So he had notes translated by the girls and passed onto me. I am sure that the girls used more subtle words in Thai than he had dictated. But all the requests and threats became more and more violent. He seemed to be obsessed with the idea of having me.

Late one evening Nid came up to me, shaking her head and saying that the Captain was prepared to pay any price for me.

"He's whining for you, and has even promised me one thousand baht if I get you for him. Why won't you do it really? There's not much that can happen to you."

"You know, I think of the axe and the bamboo, and the way they can only ever be enemies."

68

"Ah, sweetie, you really don't know much about men. You may think they're as strong as steel, but they melt like cocoa butter once you get them between your legs."

"Nid, it's not really *him*. It's more than just a question of the Captain. I see him as Captain America. Everything foreign, arrogant and power-mad. But so what! You're right. *Farang* tarts like us live off these contradictions. Tell him I'll do it tonight. Just this once and never again. Five thousand baht. Ask him where he lives and how he wants me."

I was now determined to get the night over with. Nid came back quickly.

"Here's the address. A bungalow. He liked your motorbike number. That's what you have to wear. Get it?"

I went by taxi to the bungalow, and I went in with my bag. He stood at the other end of the room. He seemed almost shy. "Where's the bathroom?" I asked. He showed me the way, and I went to change. When I came back he stared straight at me. On with the show. He looked at me as if he wanted to eat me up.

"You're so beautiful on that motorbike. So strong. So wild. So cruel!"

And then, would you believe it, he fell on his knees. So that was how it was. Captain America, the brutal, intimidating strong-man, was begging to be released from playing his role. He was wallowing in pitiful weakness. I toyed with the lash of the leather whip. It took a lot for me to whip a man for the first time in my life. But his whining and begging struck a nerve inside me, triggering off bitterness, anger and aggression which was already there. It was crazy, but true. I curled the whip round his neck and pulled him to the ground. He tore his black clothes off, revealing a body covered in a twitching and extravagant mass of tattoos. I lashed him on the back. He luxuriated in the pain, and his eyes were popping out of his head as he begged me for more. I also scourged him with words. All he could understand was my sibilant and threatening tone, since I was speaking in Thai.

"I am from the jungle. My mother is a she-panther, my father is a gibbon. My hair is a mass of slim-bodied vipers, my arms have the power of great serpents. My feet can strike with tigers' claws. A swarm of rats pursues me and they are in love with my excrement. Lizards' tongues flash from my womb. The entrance to it is guarded with the fangs of predatory beasts. Woe betide the intruding stranger."

It was a pity the Captain could not understand what I was saying. It might have turned him on even more. He wanted a strong woman, and I was a quick learner. I saw him rolling about in front of me, revelling in it, though he must have been in agonising pain. I could see the bulge in his leather briefs jerking rhythmically and finally releasing bursts of glutinous semen. Then he lay back on the teak floor, relieved, looking at me with the devotion of a baby which has just been fed from the breast. I crouched down next to him, filled with amazement.

"Doesn't it hurt?"

A stupid question. He smiled.

"Will you come again? I'll call you when the wounds have healed up and the scabs are going. I'll pay you two thousand every time you come."

I looked at him for a while, and then gave in to my instincts by wiping away the sweat on his forehead with a flannel. That is not the sort of thing a professional dominatrix is supposed to do, but I felt like it.

"OK."

I took two thousand baht from the five thousand on the table, changed my clothes, and left.

I liked to see the money in my bank account grow. At last I could send money to my family. My brothers and sisters could now lead the life I had lost. First of all I sent eight thousand baht, which would be enough for a decent water buffalo, seed and fertiliser while still leaving one thousand for other outgoings.

With the money I sent a letter which, like the payment slip, only had my name on it, no address. Besides my suggestions of ways to use the money and some fond greetings to my family I wanted to give some indication of what had become of me, of how uncertain my future was. But I left it all in the dark, and signed off with some words of optimism.

★

And what had become of my dear, cheeky, capricious Nid? She had become a rather sleepy pussy cat. And why? Because she had fallen in love with a little grey mouse. All her instincts, whether natural or acquired, seemed to have been dulled. But perhaps that was what she had always been secretly longing for, an inconspicuous life at the side of an ordinary man.

For a time Nid had not really been doing any business. It was funny to watch her trying to make herself even prettier every evening. She was not so provocative in her appearance as she had been, though she was still pretty sexy. But that was part of the ritual of love between Nid and Jim. Every evening she would pretend to be looking for business, when really she was only waiting for him. And she usually started work on pulling a trick when she knew Jim would be coming in at any moment. And every time we were treated to the same scene of jealousy. Nid jumped up as if she had been caught in the act and ran off to the lavatory. Jim put on a show of despair and jealousy and threatened his poor unknowing "rival". Then all the other girls began to play the game. They gathered round Jim and chirped in singsong pidgin:

"You no good. You no believe Nid love you. Nid no butterfly. She only love you. Leally!" Jim, who had already half forgiven Nid, would look over to the bar where she was sitting, turned away from him and powdering her nose, although anyone could see that she was really using her make-up mirror to see the expression on his face. Soon she was making eyes at him again, and they would end up spending the evening wrapped up in each other, holding hands and dancing close.

One evening I decided to speak to Nid about Jim, because we really were like sisters. We sat in a corner of the bar drinking tea. When I saw the light in her eyes I knew that anything I could say would fall on deaf ears.

"Can you remember our last evening in Udon?" she asked. "You know, I've got everything I ever wanted now. I won't be a tart any more. I'll be a respectable housewife, and I'm not too old to have kids. There are people from so many different races in America that my four slant-eyed babies won't even be noticed."

So I played along with a game whose end I did not dare try and predict. I really tried to share her joy, but doubts just kept on nagging at me. Every time I saw Jim I wondered whether he would have the guts to protect Nid in a strange world, and whether he was mature enough to think of all the problems of a marriage between races and cultures.

About two months later Nid was sitting on her packed suitcases. She had shared out her professional gear among the other girls and had bought a new wardrobe. Her shady past was forgotten, and she and Jim were already husband and wife in the eyes of the Thai law. It had been a quiet wedding, and there had been tears in the eyes of many of the girls. There was to be another celebration in the States with Jim's family and friends. He was to leave the army so he could become a mechanic again in his small hometown in the Midwest.

I felt very sad as we took the two of them to the long-distance bus for Bangkok. There was a time machine running in my head and I saw myself in twelve years' time in Nid's position. The future did not seem too rosy. We hugged each other, sobbing.

"Write soon!" I called to her as the bus took her further away.

I got the first airmail letter about four weeks later. She sent her love and described in a matter-of-fact way her new living conditions. I had just been to Udon to see the film *Paper Moon* with Pim, and we wondered whether Nid's life in a small town was like the movie.

I received letters at intervals of about three weeks, and from them I could tell that there were changes taking place in Nid's life, or at least in her perception of it. She referred more and more to the little stories about funny events, arguments and love affairs that I put in my letters. It seemed that she was sorry not to be able to take part in these happenings any more. And there did not seem to be any trace in her letters of the happiness she had felt in looking forward to her new life. Those of us left behind felt excited about her new life, but in writing about herself she was so terribly impersonal, as if she were the severe and disinterested observer of her own fate. I formed a picture in my mind of her life. It was not very appealing. A neat little wasteland of a town, like the one I had seen in *Paper Moon*. Hypocritical friendliness towards the exotic new wife. The undercurrents of competition from the prim and self-righteous white women, whispering behind their hands about what the oriental woman's job may have been before. The sly friendliness of the men, with suggestive undertones beneath the kindness.

You cannot even eat to make yourself feel better, because the food is so heavy, bland and dull that it sticks in your gullet like a lump of papier mâché and swells up there. And your husband cannot find a job and wonders whether he would not do better to go to California, but cannot find it in him to make the move. Day after day he sits in front of the TV, and does not even have the self-respect to clear away the empty beer cans. And the tacky house, all plastic, none of the warmth of wood, no feeling of being away from the street because no one takes off their shoes when they come inside. And hoping for a child, a real friend of your own. You have already missed your period twice. The doctor tells you that you are pregnant. The hormones act on your body, bringing a feeling of optimism.

In the last letter Nid sent me she told me in few words that she had lost her baby. The writing was very shaky and there were rough patches on the paper where tears had fallen.

Then I heard nothing more from her. I tried to find out if the post was on strike. I asked Jim's friends whether they had received any letters. I asked GI's on their way home to try and find out what had happened. But nothing was any good. I just clung to the hope that Nid would pull something off. She had always been so determined to sort things out.

And then one day Nid was back again. She appeared at twilight, right on time for the start of business. I was just so happy that I hugged her, my eyes stinging with tears.

But then I had a proper look at her. I took her away from the other girls and all their excited questions, and sat down with her in a quiet corner. She smiled, probably for the first time in a long while, but her smile lines hardened into bitterness. There was a hunted look in her eyes. Her hands clasped an old paper handkerchief that had already fallen to pieces. When I touched her arm she jumped.

"What's happened?" I asked, full of concern. "Tell me, please." She answered me absently, as if she did not care.

"What's there to tell? It wasn't quite what I had hoped for. I made it to San Francisco. I scraped together enough money for the flight home. You can guess how." She opened her blouse, and I was horrified to see a deep scar running between her breasts. "The pimps had it in for me. I was poaching on their territory. It was filthy work in the warehouses at the docks. Rats all around you. On oily rags. Or on your knees. You know what I mean."

I felt so sad, so desperate as I looked at her. "Listen, you must rest a while. We'll look after you. You'll have forgotten it all in a few days. We're just like a family here."

She smiled coldly. "I'm working tonight. I haven't got as much time left as you."

She would not listen to anything we had to say. It was as if, with her eyes on some distant and invisible goal, she was looking for her own destruction. She began drinking heavily, and became so difficult to deal with that she put off most of the punters. She began taking hard drugs, and her ever-decreasing income was used up on her fixes. She ran into debt all over the place, but at least I could help her there. She sank lower and lower in the men's estimation. They began to call her by a horrible nickname, *Scarslit*.

I had worked hard at placating the madame, but eventually there was nothing more to be done.

"Malee, I'm grateful to you for turning this dive into something decent. Do you want it to go to the dogs again? And something else. I've had a word with the doctor, and Nid isn't getting a "Not found" stamp on her VD-card any more. He's scared she may have the clap, maybe even Vietnam Rose – and she's allergic to penicillin."

I ran to the dormitory but Nid had gone, taking her bedding and belongings. I asked the other girls if they knew anything. One of them thought she had seen her on the way to the Reno Bar, the most disreputable of them all, where they charged twenty baht a trick.

I ran off to the end of the street. They tried to stop me at the door of the Reno, but I forced my way through. I found Nid. She had got ready for work, had too much make-up on and looked a hideous slut. I pulled her to a musty corner of the bar, which smelled of semen-smeared rags.

"Nid, you can't do this! You're not well!"

She grinned at me. "You know that they call me Scarslit. And that's my speciality. Tit-fucking with Scarslit. No one will catch anything from me that way. Anyway, I've got medicine."

She drunkenly fumbled around in her handbag, got out a pillbox and then swallowed down six capsules with whisky. Helpless to do anything, I turned away and walked despondently back up the street. I ordered a double *Gai Daeang* from the bar. I would not have been able to dance otherwise. Just as I was going to change, the doorman from the Reno Bar ran in breathlessly.

"The doctor's asking for you. Something's happened!" I took Arun's bike and roared down the street. When I got to the door, they pointed me silently upstairs. The doctor had his back to me, but when he looked at me I saw the pained expression on his face. Nid was lying on a mattress. They had closed her eyes and folded her hands. This made her look peaceful, although her face was contorted. I heard the doctor's voice as if from far away.

"She took penicillin although she was allergic to it. And the alcohol on top of that. Bad circulation, a destructive way of life . . ."

That was all I heard. I knelt beside her, looked at her hands, touched them.

"My sister . . ."

I got back onto the motor bike. Without turning the headlamp on I drove onto the highway in darkness. Women's faces came at me from every direction, the layer of make-up on their faces suddenly dissolving to reveal syphilitic decay at their nostrils.

I woke up quaking in Pim's arms.

"Did you manage without me?" She smiled reassuringly. I knew that I could not stay in Udon. We had come in search of a new life, but now Nid's death had put a curse on the place. I had seen the most terrible side of a whore's existence there. I needed to get away and have some peace so that I could sort out my own future.

"Do you understand me, Pim?" She answered me carefully.

"I've been wondering for some time whether we're in the

right place. They say that the Americans are going to leave. I'd like to go to Pattaya. Life's more peaceful there and the air's cleaner. And the tourists are better-tempered and more generous. I mean, I come from Thonburi. I know what life in Bangkok's like."

"I think I'd like to have a look around there first. And if you're in Pattaya I can visit you. I wouldn't like us to lose touch."

I got in the bus around noon the next day. I was grateful to the madame for being so understanding, even though it meant she would lose by it. The girls were very sweet when we said good-bye, and I went off feeling very depressed.

We left the plateau of the Isan, and with it my home region, and drove down onto the central plain which has Bangkok at its centre.

A Tiger growling inside

Bangkok

As a peasant's daughter from the Isan, I was amazed by the fertile rice-fields of the central flood plain. How could people go hungry when there was this endless tapestry of rice fields running from one horizon to another?

The individual fields grew bigger as we approached Bangkok. The day was ending. On the left appeared the lights of Don Muang airport, and the bus was soon caught up in slow traffic as it made its way towards the northern bus station in Pahonyotin Street.

I was dazed by all the new impressions, the exhaust fumes and the roar of the traffic. My gestures were sluggish as I took my luggage from the station and loaded it into a taxi. I found out that the taxi driver was also from the Isan; he wanted to go home for the harvest and help his family on their little farm. He lived the life of a vagabond, snatching exhausted sleep on the plastic seat in the back of the rickety car he rented. What he told me made me sad. Why wasn't it possible to lead the simple life of a peasant any more, in peace and sufficiency? In Ploenchit Street the taxi turned off shortly after it had crossed the railway into the Soi Nanatai. Pim had given me the address of a cousin of hers, a girl working in the Los Angeles Bar. The customers there were nearly all foreigners, since there were a lot of three and four-star hotels in the area.

Business had already started in the bar, but luckily Pim's cousin Amon had not picked a customer up yet. I gave her a letter, and this made her only too ready to help me. One of the barmen was also the manager. I would have preferred a woman, but the working atmosphere seemed to be tougher here. He looked me up and down and clicked his tongue. Not a good start. I would have to be careful of him.

Also, I was not happy that there was only a tiny platform in the middle of the room for one go-go girl, and no real stage. There was no way you could keep your distance from the men.

I asked Amon about the prices. Three or four hundred a night minus the hefty sum for the bar manager.

"But you're so pretty," she said, "it'll be easy for you to get an extra tip."

I still didn't like the look of things, and decided to search out other possibilities. All the same, I had somewhere to stay and I did not have to work that night.

The next day I studied the plan of the town, acquainted myself with the major bus routes and asked the girls how much taxis cost to various important places. They told me that the price depended not on distance, but on the traffic. I also found out about how to get to the Menam Khaopraya, because I was particularly looking forward to seeing the earth-coloured river.

Then I looked around the neighbourhood, from Siam Square with its shops in one direction, to the grand Erawan Hotel in the other. This hotel was one of the few in Bangkok which does not like "overnight guests" in the form of prostitutes. I heard, though, that many guests came to the Los Angeles Bar from the hotel, took another room, this time in Nanatai Street, and only turned up again at their official hotel for breakfast.

I began to get ready for the evening, but I did not feel right. What had happened in Udon still filled my thoughts, although an awful lot seemed to have happened since Pim's death. My lack of enthusiasm for work was reflected in the ordinary look I adopted that evening: a knee-length pleated skirt, flat shoes, and a very demurely cut blouse buttoned up to the neck like a schoolgirl. My hair was up in a bun and I was not even wearing any lip-gloss. The manager looked at me disapprovingly and muttered:

"I didn't know this was a place for good girls. But perhaps you'll make a go of it."

I did not always find it offputting when men looked me up and down. When I felt strong, secure and in charge of the situation, being sized up did not bother me at all. It was all part of the business: goods in return for money. And of course I tried to attract the attention of the customers by presenting my wares in a particular way, so as to interest them and make them want to buy. The more they desired me, the readier they would be to pay a good price. And if they were really slavering after me, then the level of negotiation could be higher. It was all a simple matter of economics.

But it was not like that tonight. I felt so much a mere cog in the machinery of prostitution that I could not let my imagination go. And, of course, some guy had his eye on me already, even though, as I noticed with exasperation, there were plenty of girls free. Then the manager called to me:

"He's a regular. Don't put him off. I wouldn't have thought he'd go for your get-up. Perhaps he can see through it . . ."

I was in a really bad mood by now. The suggestive comments from the man behind the bar and my "professional obligations" were the last straw.

Now it was my turn to look the customer up and down and I did not like what I saw. He was about one metre seventy tall, stocky, paunchy, wearing a "tropical" shirt which was soaked with sweat. His fairish hair was thin, and he had greasy skin with red freckles. I have nothing against ugly people, but at that particular moment I would have liked to have called out angrily to him:

"Can't you see how stupid this is? You are more than twice my age, flabby, drunk, bleary-eyed, stupid – and so damn full of yourself. And I'm young, pretty, slim and graceful, with a glow in my eye and a luscious mouth which I can use to drive a lover wild. My skin is firm and soft, and gleams gently in the dim light. My thoughts can fly as free as a flamingo. But you're the one with the money and the power. You ought to be my slave, but you see yourself as the master."

How repulsive he was! He spoke English with a harsh accent, and, like many of the men in the bar, was a German. He proudly told me he worked for Heckler and Koch. "Weapons, you know. Bang, bang!" He laughed as if he had made a joke. I would gladly have shoved a prickly cactus into his great big mouth. He was touching me up already, groping under my skirt, and began to go on about how young I was. He wanted something very special.

"Oh yeah, in Thailand they've got girls who've hardly been touched. Not worn-out old scrubbers like back home. They really fall in love with you."

I was to become all too familiar with this story.

When he tried to feel about between my buttocks I went in for the attack. I hurried him on, because I wanted to get it all over with. He was so stupid and sure of himself that he thought I was looking forward to it, and he hastily finished his beer.

We took a short taxi ride to the Reno Hotel. The warm air combined with the drink was making him sleepy, and I had to rouse him at the hotel entrance. I defied the looks of the hotel staff as we walked through the lounge. He had rented a room for a long stay, but not a single book or flower was in evidence to brighten up the impersonal coldness of the standard guest room. I went onto the balcony and looked down into the

electric blue water of the swimming pool, plunging deep
down in my thoughts, passing through cool underground
channels to reach the sea and freedom. Then I pulled myself
together and went back to the bedroom.

The punter had taken his clothes off and was now lying with
his fat body spreading all over the bed. His watery eyes
hardened a little as he fixed them on me. With my back to him
I undressed as quickly as I could so that he would not think I
was in the least enthusiastic about the job. When I finally
turned to him I saw that his eyes were glued to my bottom. So
that was what he wanted. I lay down on my stomach and froze
as his trembling middle finger slipped from my coccyx deep
into the furrow of my behind. I thought of Nid's fighting
spirit with clients. Hesitatingly I murmured:

"The strong man is tired tonight. Let's spoil him a little. Lie
on your back. I'll make it good for you."

With a sigh of pleasure he did as I said. I squatted over his
crotch, took hold of his pathetic little organ, clenched it in my
backside and exerted a quick burst of pressure with my back
muscles. Now, I do not know whether I had eaten too much
chilli, or perhaps I was suffering from wind, but I suddenly
exploded in an enormous fart. And he *loved* it. It drove him
crazy! His penis jumped and jerked and finally squirted onto
his great wobbly belly.

I went hot and cold. I was filled with disgust, but I also felt
like bursting into laughter. I ran into the bathroom and
drenched myself under the shower. When I got back to the
bedroom he was asleep already. I got dressed and left without
my money. I just had to get away.

It was business as usual in the bar. I spoke to the manager:

"Don't worry. Everything's all right. He was just a bit tired
tonight." Then I said, "And I'd like time off tomorrow,
because I have to visit my sick aunt." He did not look too
happy, but said nothing.

I had a beer to calm me down, but I spent the night tossing in
my sleep.

A Tiger growling inside

The rays of the new day brushed softly against me. It was early on Saturday morning, and there were not many cars about. The air almost seemed to be pure and clear.

I had put a change of panties and a toothbrush in my handbag, and I took a taxi almost as far as the Tatien pier. I made my way towards the pier through the confusion of people, noises and smells in the dimly lit hall of the big market. Leaving the sweaty coolies and the strident Chinese women behind me I came to the river. The "Mother of the Waters" lay in front of me, bathed in light, seemingly laden with fruitfulness, life-giving moisture and the rich, thick mud which gave it the evocative colour of milky coffee. On the Thonburi side stood the Wat Arun, silhouetted against the light. Tough little tugs were like the heads of flexible lizards whose jointed bodies were made up of heavy transport sampans. The wood of these boats had been faded by the sun and water to a dun colour, but they were brightened by the vivid shades of the washing hung out to dry by the families who lived on them. Sliding along between them were sleek, high-speed sampans, built in valuable woods. They had powerful motors and long propeller shafts designed to get to the furthest corners of the canal system, even the silted-up end of a *klong* where water-hyacinths would get caught up in the blades. And then there were other little sampans pushed along with a pole. There were mainly women on them, wearing straw peasants' hats and selling delicacies. And floating everywhere there were balls of vegetation made of leaves and lianas which had been torn away from their mother-plants by the tropical rains. When we were children we used to play hide and seek in them, in spite of our parents' warnings about the snakes that often lived there.

I sat down on one of the bollards on the pier and slowly took in the scene. A sense of peace returned within me. I wanted time to think, but what seemed important to me now was to listen to the murmur of the river, and to let the rhythm of my blood and thoughts become one with its flow. I was back in time with the ancient pace of our culture, our civilisation which owes everything to the power and generosity of water.

I woke from my reverie as the ship's bell rang for the first time. I joined the queue to get on the boat going to Ayuddhaya. The sampan was several times the size of traditional boats, being able to take about fifty passengers, but it was built in the old way, long and narrow with a very shallow draught. The adjustable propeller was on an extension away from the stern, and the motor was in the open at the back of the boat. Like the rest of the sampan, it was brightly polished and had a well-tended oily gleam. Even the cylinders were chromed. It had an air of mystery and power, but at the same time seemed benign and trustworthy.

The queue was moving, and I had already taken several steps down to the boat when I caught my right foot and lost my balance. It looked like it could have been the end of my day out, but suddenly I felt an arm around me. A broad flat chest was pressed against my back and my bottom came down onto a knee. The scent of after-shave rushed into my nostrils and a deep voice boomed in my ear:

"But you aren't even wearing a bathing suit!"

It was a terrible joke, but everyone laughed happily, mainly because the man who had made it was a *farang*. I was back on both feet by now, and he relaxed his grip. I turned to him and apologised, using the polite word "*Garuna*". Then I found my place in the queue again.

It somehow turned out that we ended up sitting next to each other, so I could take a look at him for the first time. He was slim, but looked strong too. His clothes were simple, but not sloppy like so many foreigners'. He was wearing pale linen trousers and a dark blue peasant-style shirt, which was actually made of silk. His dark blond hair was thick, healthy and curly. His skin was evenly tanned, again unusual for a *farang*, and his whitish-blond body hair shimmered against it. There seemed to be a slightly ironic expression in the corners of his mouth, which I took to mean that he was not condescending by nature. For a moment his eyes looked deep into mine. I was taken aback, because I had never seen anyone with green eyes before. I also noticed that his Adam's apple was moving up and down, betraying the inner tension behind his apparent calm. Seeing that made me feel more sure of myself.

He seemed to be enjoying the trip as much as I was. We stayed silent most of the time, taking everything in. The boat went from side to side of the river to reach the various mooring points. I admired the way the helmsman steered the stern so skilfully into the jetty that there was no need to tie up, and passengers getting on or off did not risk falling in either.

The stops were often made in front of schools and temples, where passengers waited in a small *sala*. As the boat quickly approached the bank we saw for a moment into the private life of the river dwellers, whose houses of faded reddish-grey teak rose out of the water on stilts. From close to we saw people sitting on the steps down to the river and washing themselves. Women were crouching in the porches facing the river, preparing food or producing handiwork. Naked children were shouting and jumping into the water. Their wet skin gleamed as the sun caught it. Even as we were approaching they called "Goodbye" in English to the *farang* at my side. It was probably the only word they knew. He waved back every time.

I found him more and more surprising. Seeing me looking at the banks of the river with such untiring curiosity, he obviously felt obliged to provide a commentary:

"That's the Phraram-Hog Bridge. Over there to the left is the mouth of the Bang Kruat canal."

He interrupted our pensive silence more and more regularly. I was happy to listen to him, because I liked the way he, a foreigner, knew so much about it all.

"Over there you can see the North Bangkok Power Station. It's linked by the grid to all the other power stations and dams in the country. Only a very small proportion of the generating power is being used at the moment. The generator is on full power at night." He laughed. "Back home in Germany where I come from it's the other way round. More power is used during the day."

"Why's that?" I asked.

"Because Thailand is less industrial. The current is used mostly in the evening for lighting. At home we use much more energy for industry."

I thought about this for a while, and then asked him what his job was.

"I'm working as an advisor at the Asian Institute of Technology. I've got about another year to go."

He seemed to be a little sad at the prospect of having to leave. Even as I asked him the next question I wished I had not.

"Are you here with your family?"

There was a touch of melancholy in his eyes as he answered me.

"No. I live here alone."

He stayed thinking for a while. I did not say much either. Eventually he tried to start off the conversation again with a light-hearted remark.

"Do you want to go to Bang Pa In? We could take a taxi there together." This was not the sort of thing to ask a nice young lady. I glanced at my clothes. My dusky pink silk dress with copper-coloured stitching at the edges was closely cut and elegant, but really a bit old-fashioned. There was nothing suspicious about my appearance or my behaviour. Perhaps it was just that he did not want me to disappear straight out of his life. This thought made me feel closer to him. I smiled at him hesitantly, saying, "That seems a very sensible idea." After all, it seemed only reasonable to do things together since we obviously had the same itinerary planned for the weekend.

By now we were on polite first-name terms. I was glad that

his name was easy for a Thai to pronounce. In fact it sounded good. *Khun* Benjamin had already been to Bang Pa In, but he seemed to be as taken with the beauty of this pavilion on the lake as I was. The *sala* in filigree wood stands on a pillared platform made of semi-precious stone. Legend has it that King Chulalongkon built it in memory of his wife, who died when her boat capsized. I was lost in the world of this romantic story, and only after a little while did I notice that he was standing close to me. So close, that an electric charge was passing between the hairs on our arms.

Towards evening we went to Ayuddhaya and each took a room in the U Thong Hotel. We arranged to meet in half an hour at a nearby bar.

The restaurant opened onto the street. The warm evening air was transformed by the electric fans into a refreshing breeze. There were tempting smells floating about. We were both hungry, and full of anticipation of our meal we suggested various dishes to each other.

One of my favourite starters came first: pigs' ears marinated in soy sauce, roasted and served cold. With it was *nem*, a refreshing pork sausage, spicy and tangy, and beef salad. Then two charcoal-filled "steamboats" were brought to the table. Simmering in them were two bowls of soup flavoured with lemon grass: one had chicken as its main ingredient, the other, freshwater crayfish. These soups served as an accompaniment to the main dishes: rice in coconut milk with pawpaw salad, beef with salad in oyster sauce, pork stir-fried with garlic, onions and sweet and sour fish.

There was a lot to eat, and we had to finish off with a little drink of Chinese *gaoliang* so that our pleasant tiredness after a good meal did not turn into sleepiness.

Neither of us wanted to stop talking. Our conversation had been so easy during dinner, with a quiet sense of intimacy, discreetly affectionate curiosity about each other, and flirtatious, almost loving questions and little word games.

We decided to go for another walk, and found an overgrown and magical spot on the river, which was gleaming at our feet, dreaming in the moonlight. I am terribly sentimental, and at that instant I would have been ready to hang myself on a moonbeam so that I would never have to lose the beauty of the moment.

"You're crazy," I said to myself. "You don't know what you're doing." Benjamin turned to me. He cleared his throat, but his voice still sounded hoarse.

"Malee, please, just for a moment . . ."

He drew me to him, his soft lips caressed mine, trying with a hint of desperation to find their way in to the limitless welcome that was waiting. Our bodies wrapped around each other. The buds of my breasts sprang up, as if to burrow into his chest, swelling to fill the space they had made. He pressed the hardness in his crotch against my vulva. It would have taken him in, if I had not suddenly torn myself away.

You whore, you damn whore!

We were both in a state of confusion as we made our way back to the hotel. Before we reached the street and its lights, I took hold of his hand and smiled. "I'm looking forward to tomorrow."

We said a formal and embarrassed goodnight to each other, as if we were trying to protect ourselves with good manners.

We had ordered a *tuk-tuk* to pick us up from the hotel at nine the next morning. *Tuk-tuk* is the onomatopoeic name for a motorised tricycle rickshaw with a low covering on top. *Tuk-tuks* are airier – and cheaper – than taxis, but a careless driver taking a corner too quickly can easily turn over.

For four hundred and fifty years Ayuddhaya was the capital of Siam, until their arch-enemy, the Burmese burned it down in 1767. The town never recovered from the fire and Thonburi-Bangkok became the main city in Siam.

How glorious court life in Ayuddhaya must have been, when even Cambodia was a dominion of Siam. At the court conversation was often in improvised verse, and many of the princes were also poets. But for all the art and power, life was based on a simple economical and philosophical principle: "There is rice in the fields, there are fish in the water."

All the royal splendour depended on the rice farmers, but they performed their tasks according to a social contract which also expected the ruling class to do its duty, especially in matters of irrigation and the military protection of the independent village communities. And the decadent aristocrats eventually forgot to fulfil their part of the bargain. When the Burmese were advancing, the brave General Daksin fired cannons in defence, but the king wanted to have him executed for shocking the delicate nerves of the courtiers by not warning them beforehand.

So the huge and sprawling palaces and temples of once glorious Ayuddhaya have now been in ruins for more than two hundred years. The only life there since has been blasphemous temple robbers, the invading tendrils of nature and the breath of history. The temple robbers, reincarnated as snakes and geckos, are doomed never to leave the scene of their crime.

Benjamin sensed that I was bringing the past back to life, putting all these ruins back as they once were, wandering through the palace dressed in the brocade of a princess, or offering up flowers as a modest peasant girl in the temple. He smiled a little, only touching me occasionally, as if by chance.

The hours passed and it was time to go back. After all, I had to work that evening. Suddenly it was time to return to the world I had been able to forget almost completely for the last two days.

We took the bus back to town, both of us wrapped up in our own thoughts and feelings hardly exchanging a word. We were soon caught up in heavy traffic on the outskirts of Bangkok. The exhaust fumes were suffocating. I was absolutely miserable. Benjamin was getting restless. We were going to have to say goodbye soon. Turning half towards me, his eyes sank to the floor.

"Malee, I don't know if I should tell you the things I want to say. Perhaps I've got it all wrong, and what I say will just annoy you. You may even not like what you hear at all. But we have been very close to each other the last two days. I think it'd be crazy for me to have to leave you just like that."

I looked at him, almost shaking with apprehension. Of course I wanted to tell him how I felt. But I was a whore, and I was afraid he would reject me if he found that out. He might even be disgusted by it. And then I would hate him, and these two happy days would be in ruins like the city of Ayuddhaya.

I tried to find some way out. Then something took hold of me, a fire inside which made me blurt out to him:

"I'd like to see you again too. This evening. Come to this address at nine o'clock."

At the next stop I got out of the bus and took a taxi to the bar. I took no notice of the manager, who looked meaningfully at his watch as I came in. I absently exchanged a few friendly words with Amon. I did not have a lot of time. I had a shower, then put cream on my skin to make it shine. I pulled on a shiny black leotard, which was backless and sleeveless and exposed the edge of my nipples. I rolled on seamed black stockings dotted with tiny stars. Then I put on some skintight hot pants in smooth, black leather, which were just too closely cut for comfort when I moved. I patted myself on the bottom, enjoying the firmness beneath the soft leather. I completed the outfit with high-heeled ankle boots, which did not quite hide the fine chains around my ankles. Then I blow-dried my hair into a windswept style and covered my lips with gloss. Before I slipped on my short and supple leather gloves I put a delicate silver chain round my neck.

It was time to go to the bar.

I took no notice of the manager's suggestive comments, even

though he was probably trying to be appreciative. I sat down on a stool and fixed my eyes on the door. I was panting with excitement, bursting through the leotard. I could not bear to wait long. Would he hate me or love me? It was now or never.

Suddenly he was in the doorway. I slid from the stool and stood before him with my legs slightly astride. It was like the showdown of a western. I tossed back a strand of hair and placed my hands on my hips. He came up to me, as if under a spell. His face betrayed all his feelings. Amazement, disbelief, fear. But then I saw something in his eyes that I had seen once before, a warm gleam, veiled with emotion, turning it into a beautiful glow. Suddenly I was in his arms and he was stammering in my ear:

"Go on. Get your stuff. Everything. I'll talk to the manager."

I ran into the dormitory like an excited child, grabbed haphazardly at my things, threw them into my big suitcase and quickly put on a big teeshirt and a pair of linen trousers. I was incredibly relieved when I saw him again. I hugged Amon wildly, then he took me by the hand, and led me out of the bar to call a taxi.

★

His flat was in Sapphankwai in one of the *intamara* side streets of the Tanon Suttisan. He took me lovingly into the apartment, which had four big rooms, a bathroom, a kitchen and a balcony. I felt at ease straight away. It was furnished with cleverly designed dark-stained teak. The wooden floor was covered with Chinese silk rugs. There were curved rattan bookshelves with more books than I had ever seen in one place. The pictures on the walls were painted in a flat, naive style on coarse handmade paper with a very high wood content, and were mounted in midnight blue silk. They all showed scenes from rural life, which made me feel even more at home. There were plants and flowers everywhere, on the balcony too, bringing a feeling of the jungle to the city. On the big bed in the bedroom was a patchwork quilt made by the mountain tribes of the Meo. It all looked very cosy. The study was dominated by a fold-out bureau. On it was a collection of large-bowled pipes, whose smell gave the room its attractively masculine feel. The living room was divided into two, with a dining area leading onto the balcony and a sitting room furnished with luxuriously upholstered armchairs and couches, also covered in dark blue silk. The fourth room was smaller than the others, but very homely. Two luxuriant plants stood on either side of an elegant writing table at the window.

"Your room," he said proudly, knowing I would be pleased.

I began putting my things in the wardrobe straight away. He tried to stop me, but I gently shooed him away.

"Off you go. I'll be along in a minute."

He played the hurt child and wandered off. I smiled to myself.

When I went back into the bedroom the only light on in there was set amongst the plants, and it cast a blurred shadow like a jungle landscape on the wall. He was lying naked on the bed, with only a *pakomah* lying loose over his middle. I liked this little indication of modest restraint. I took off my shirt and trousers, and approached him in my sexy gear from the bar. The soft light traced the outlines of his muscles. I was longing for his embrace and knew that he could hardly breathe for excitement. I wanted to seduce him, to use all my skills, but at the same time I knew that was unnecessary. We were attracted to one another like opposing magnetic poles. I slipped out of my clothes and our bodies met each other with a shattering force, yet we were moving as lightly as down, every action in slow motion. There was no preliminary reconnaissance, just ravenous hunger. I felt all my pores, membranes and orifices opening up, waiting to be discovered, explored with his tongue. My juices began to flow. When at last he entered me he slid deeply in, holding tight onto my upper arms. I sucked him in, would not release him, stroked him and squeezed him with my contractions, opened so wide that he was lost in a void, then took hold of him again, shooting myself through with exquisite pain. Our voices joined in a duet which had only one word: *tirak*, my love. The melody was spread over many octaves, from the deepest bass to the shrillest soprano. The final notes were wildly pitched, moaning, shrieking, piercing, but to us they were like heavenly music.

The night breeze brushed over our closely entwined bodies, evaporating the sweat in our hair, bringing our senses back to earth. The feeling had been insanely strong. It was good just to think of it. I wanted to be even closer to him, but that was impossible, unless we could have been fused into one.

He seemed to be somewhere else, although his lips were close to my ear and his arms and legs were wrapped around mine. Then his broken voice found its old purity, and in soft, velvety tones, he told me a story. At first I did not understand that it was about me.

"There is a woman whose hair is long and heavy, yet it floats as lightly as the fingers of a sea anenome. Her body is as smooth and cool as a fish, but strong, electric, and with powerful and quick reactions when you touch it. Her arms and legs ensnare you and squeeze you like an octopus. Her purple lips rhythmically spray clouds of ink before your eyes, and you no longer know where you are. Her eyes shower you with light to guide you through the darkness. And her womb pulls you down deep, swallows you up, playfully pretends to release you halfway. And how awful it would be if she really did let you go!"

I got a shock when I woke the next morning to find myself alone. But then I saw some flowers lying on the pillow and a note in slightly awkward Thai script, saying:

"I'm at the office. And this evening will seem a terribly long time away."

I ran the back of my hand over the coolness of the sheet next to me. Through the curtain of leaves at the window came rays of sunlight, which formed shimmering patches of light on the dark silk of the pillow-case. I stretched pleasurably, stroked my skin, reminding my body of what it had experienced the night before. I smoothed my pubic hair and felt the surge of blood through my vulva. I slapped my other hand over my wayward fingers, and jumped up, laughing.

The bathroom was spacious and had a western-style shower as well as a basin and ladle. I stood breezily beneath the shower, at the same time ladling water over my head. My body wanted to burst with well-being. Then I went to my wardrobe and found a Hawaiian blouse in tones of olive green and yellow, and a simply-cut black skirt. These clothes were very *supab*, but sheerly enough cut, I hoped, to make him notice.

In the kitchen I found plenty of spices and utensils, but not much in the way of fresh food. So I went to the shop on the corner of our street and Suttisan Street and bought two boxes full of groceries from the Chinese there. A shopgirl, who spoke the Isan dialect, brought the things round to the flat in a trolley. I was so busy putting everything away that I almost missed hearing the telephone. His voice sounded relieved.

"I tried to get in touch with you earlier. I was scared that you'd gone . . ."

"Don't be silly! I'll stay all year if you want."

I was frightened for a moment, then his voice came quietly, as if from far away.

"Yes."

What had made me limit our time together to the year that he still had in Thailand? Was I so much of a whore that I could only see in terms of time and money? Did I consider myself so much a prostitute that I could not imagine deep and durable ties? Or was it the self-contempt of a whore who is not allowed to hope for lasting love from a man?

Then I remembered the sad look in his eyes when he answered my question on the boat to Ayuddhaya: "I live here alone." He was being honest with me, because I had felt straight away that he was only available for a specific time. How could it possibly have been that a confident, successful and attractive man still had no ties at the age of thirty-three?

Then I came to an exciting decision. I would not get maudlin about it all, and I was not going to be disappointed. I was not a princess who had been set free for a year, only to return afterwards to the dark demons' cave, there to be defiled and impaled. Until now I had always managed to find a way out and to stand on my own two feet. In the mud of the freshly-broken earth lies the seed of a new rice-shoot. I was independent, confident and optimistic. I had made up my own mind to spend a year living with a man. And I had nothing to lose.

On the contrary, I would take advantage of his tenderness and love by letting my imagination run riot, by making the most of my body. I would sound out the depths of my feelings using the measure of my devotion to him – and all the signals would come back to me. We would also agree a contract as if I were a prostitute, the economic agreement of a temporary husband and wife. And I would learn and learn and learn. Especially languages, so I could break through the barriers of the unknown.

I had never felt so strong before. When he came home I was glowing with pride, but there was a tender gleam in my eye. Did I seem strange to him at that moment? I embraced him lovingly.

"Shall we go for something to eat?" I asked.

He seemed full of uncertainty, almost resistant as I led him away.

On the Tanon Suttisan, at the level of the third *intamara* street there is a little restaurant that was to become our regular haunt. It stands on stilts in a pond full of aquatic plants. A narrow bridge is suspended over the water leading to the kitchen in the middle of the pond, and there are other bridges leading from it to the little islands where the tables are. We sat at the furthest table, surrounded by plants and the complacent croaking of invisible frogs. I bathed my eyes in the beam of light coming from above the table.

He leaned forward too and I told him about my life until then. I made no secret of how much it meant to me to have met him. And then I gave him an idea of what I had been thinking about after we had spoken on the telephone.

"We've got a year, a whole year for each other. Do you understand what I mean?"

I think he was happy, but he seemed perplexed as he took me by the hand. His face clouded over. He wanted to come clean with me, but he did not quite have it in him yet to trust me to understand.

That night we came together as man and woman in a primeval encounter. Enmity and fear turned into fascination. We fought with each other, as if we had never experienced such animal closeness before. And we licked each other as if we were trying to make up for a deficiency of salt in our own bodies.

In my life with Benjamin I was as beautiful as the tigerfish, as solicitous as the cormorant and as faithful as the crane. I loved the life I was leading, but I did not pretend it was going to last forever. My feelings for him were deep and sincere, but there was another materialistic side to them. In its purest and most pristine form, prostitution means that a woman can be full of romance and devotion and still have her material security and independence in view. Creature comforts did not mean all that much to me, but I knew that a woman could have neither respect nor free-

96

dom without the protective armour of materialism.

On our second day together I opened a new bank account and transferred my savings into it. Benjamin set up a standing order so that in addition to the housekeeping money I got eight thousand baht. Of course, that was a lot more than I would have been paid for doing my bit of housework! But it expressed something else. He knew how important it was that his home, and I as part of it, should contribute to the quality and creativity of his work.

There was an old wooden house near our block of flats where an old Chinese lived. He had a large mole on his left cheek, and sprouting from it were three long white hairs, which he played with all the time. Every time I went past his house I saw him sitting in his doorway, with his legs tucked underneath his stool, sipping tea. I had greeted him respectfully several times, when one day he paid me a lovely compliment:

"How pretty the hibiscus is, blooming in the middle of the road!"

We got talking, and he modestly told me that before his retirement he had been an English lecturer at the Thammasat University. What a piece of luck! I began to chatter away, because an idea had just occurred to me. I managed to phrase a question in respectful and well-chosen words:

"*Ayan*, one of the great gifts of age is to be untroubled by what is unworthy. But would you be ready to take an ungifted pupil and kindly teach her English? She would do her best to learn and bother you as little as possible."

The old man's eyes lit up. It probably was not just that I had expressed my respect for him. He probably needed a little variety in his life too. We soon came to an agreement.

When Benjamin came in that evening he could see straight away that I had something to tell him, and this made him smile.

"Guess what, I'm going to have private English lessons from an old university lecturer. Every morning I'll get up and go out of the flat with you. I'm having lessons from half past seven to ten, except at weekends." It was sweet of him not to make fun of my childish excitement: he knew how much I wanted to learn.

"*Tirak*, you're going to have to start virtually from the beginning again. You'll have to forget nearly all the bits and pieces you learned in Udon so that you can learn the real English language properly. And you'll have to get used to the Latin alphabet."

That night as we were making love he stopped for a moment, and looked at me with a touch of apprehension. I pulled him close to me and whispered in his ear.

"You must share my anticipation with me today. I feel for you, and I want you very much, but my feelings at the moment are swaying back and forth – with you one moment, and somewhere else the next . . ."

As he drifted off to sleep I heard him murmur:

". . . and it'll be German next."

I can still remember my first school book, *Banya le Renu bai rongrien* (Banya and Renu go to school). I can see myself running my index finger over the rounded letters of Thai script, desperate to learn them and fix them in my memory. And now years later my venerable Chinese teacher was smiling at my impatient desire for knowledge.

"It is much easier to write in Latin letters than Thai ones. Western script only has twenty-six letters, while Thai has thirty-two vowels to start with, and then twenty-one consonants. So that puts us at an advantage straight away."

I soon became very fond of my old teacher. He was quietly authoritative and put quite heavy demands on me, which fired my ambition still further. He never praised me, but I could tell he was happy with my progress because he sped up the rate of the lessons and he began to treat me like a friend. I was as happy about this as I was about the enthusiastic praise I got from Benjamin – although he did sometimes tease me by saying I had a parrot's gift for learning languages.

We spent many quiet evenings at home. The monsoon rain poured down outside, weighing down the leaves of the plants on the balcony, while the plants inside moved in the gentle, cooling breeze, and we would lie cushioned in the comfortable furniture in the living-room. Benjamin liked traditional Thai music played on wooden instruments, and had a large collection of records and tapes. Now and then I would throw a few things into a wok on the stove, toss them over the flame and serve a tasty little snack. Meanwhile, Benjamin liked to test me on my vocabulary and try to trick me with difficult sentences. And I could use him as a walking dictionary. My vocabulary was growing quickly, and difficult concepts were coming in, ones which I had perhaps only heard on the rare occasion when they were thrown into a Thai conversation: ecology, emancipation, atheism, anarchy. I was so pleased and grateful when he patiently and imaginatively put them in context for me. The involvement in his face and the expressive gestures of his hands sometimes even excited me. Then I would stretch out, looking at him dreamily and just a little mockingly, pushing my breasts forward, maybe stroking them with an absent gesture, and trying all sorts of other tricks. I could have burst out into delighted laughter when he lost track of what he was saying, and began to stammer and blush like an adolescent. Then he would call me "Salome". I liked that name, which he had explained to me after our first time . . .

We often felt like going out too. We would take Benjamin's car or a taxi to Chinatown, where we would go to a (respectable) Turkish bath. There the employees worked at our fat and our muscles until the combination of sweating and massage made our skin look translucent. Then we went to feed ourselves back up again with a big meal in one of the high-class Chinese restaurants. Back home we made love. Each time we moved we were shot through with delicious pain, which made us moan continually. It made me laugh to imagine what anyone listening would think!

Sometimes we went to the Tatien pier, to "our" river. We would hire a small sampan and be taken to Nonthaburi, by which time it was usually twilight. Then the sampan would take us back downstream with the motor chugging gently, and we would look at the rows of lights along the riverbanks.

On several occasions we went to the chaotic Rajdamnoen Stadium to place our bets on Thai boxing. I had a better eye for the fighters than Benjamin, and I won much more often than he did. Although he was able to send himself up very easily, I do not think he was all that happy about my expertise in assessing men's bodies. He would remain bad-tempered until I took him reassuringly by the hand. But I must say that I enjoyed his jealousy. The seething noises of cheers, gongs and exciting music of the band, together with the competitive atmosphere made my blood rush. On those nights I took no notice of Benjamin's sexual desires, and he became the submissive partner in our love-play.

Often, though, we would just go to our little island of bamboo at the restaurant in the pond. We had become regular customers and would spend quiet evenings there, but they were full of animated and exhilarating conversation. We spoke openly, getting to know each other even better. He had been to nearly all the countries in Europe at least once, and his traveller's tales aroused ever greater curiosity in me.

We usually left the polluted air of Bangkok on a Friday afternoon. During our first weekends together Benjamin had, of course, taken me to see some more of the sights in the city such as the floating market (*dalad nam*) in Thonburi, the weekend market (*sanam luang*) near the Thammasat, the National Museum and the major temples. But after five days in Bangkok your lungs thirst for a breath of fresh air, and we would take a bus, a train or the car to escape the shroud of smog.

We sometimes went inland for the weekend, to Kanchanaburi or the bridge on the River Kwai, but we generally preferred the sea. Several times we went to Hua Hin, the classic Thai seaside resort, where we stayed in the lovely old Railway Hotel.

When we took these trips out of Bangkok I chose to dress with restrained elegance, mostly wearing traditional silk clothes, and since we spoke Thai together we were taken to be a respectable couple, and I was not suspected of being a whore with her *farang*.

The furthest away we went was about thirty kilometres beyond Rayong towards the Cambodian border. A business-man – Chinese, of course – had built some bungalows there. We were the only people staying there. Two provincial pimps with three very young girls came looking for a pick-up since they had heard there was a foreigner around. But they did not stay for long once they saw me.

In itself the beach was very picturesque, with palm trees fringing the brilliant white sand, but the place was dirty. The fishermen used it for their work, and there was all sorts of rubbish lying around: rotting coconut shells, forlorn fish-heads, bits of plastic bag, even a dead dog. We were so disappointed that we considered going back to Pattaya, but then Benjamin saved the day. There was a gang of curious children nearby. He called to them and gave three baht to each of them, even a tiny one still sucking his thumb. The children found some large baskets and within an hour the sand was spotless as far as the eye could see. The little toddler had been particularly keen to help, although he could not really be a lot of use.

The weather was dry and sunny, but there were big waves in the Gulf of Siam. The fishermen were having trouble loading their catch. I love the breakers and I ran into them where they broke on the shore, and was left gasping by the shower of spray. Benjamin got beyond the surf and swam a little way out to sea, then turned back, swimming hard trying

101

to keep up with the biggest wave until it crashed on the shore, taking him with it. He was good at body-surfing, but sometimes tried his luck rather too far, ending up being pushed onto the sand and grazing his chest. This did not stop me from swimming out time after time to learn how to surf. I was physically exhausted, but I was drunk with the foam as if in a sea of champagne.

That Saturday evening we sat down to eat with the fishermen at a little restaurant (if you could call it that) among the palm trees by the sea. There was a kitchen with a roof of leaves and some rough tables and chairs which were stuck into the sand. But the food was delicious. We had several helpings of fresh grilled fish with rice, and sweet and sour fish soup. We shared fermented coconut milk with the fishermen. Benjamin asked them whether the Malaysian and Japanese trawlers ever came in to their fishing territory, and so began a lively discussion which became more and more heated under the influence of the alcohol.

We lay in bed that night in our bungalow which was built on stilts over the surf. Our bodies moved to the deep rolling rhythm of the waves, with a heavier thrust at each third wave, then an even more passionate one at the seventh. The sap of our love foamed, bubbled and eddied like the sea around the stilts of the house. All I could see was a shimmering veil of foam before my eyes, I was being carried up, high up, and then brought softly back to land by the gentle billows.

Pim had been good about writing letters, but then I went for four weeks without hearing anything from her. Eventually a fat letter arrived from her in Pattaya. She sounded relieved and happy. She had left the sinking ship just in time. There were reports in the papers about Udon, saying that the Americans had moved out, just leaving a few essential telecommunications personnel. A whole brigade of camp-followers was left without an army, and they were now all over the country looking for a new place to go.

Pim was now working the Fantasy Club in Pattaya. It is a real sex supermarket, with loads of girls on the lookout for customers every evening, buying a "permit" from the management with a twenty-five baht drinks coupon. The club has a long room, with the bar to the right of the entrance and then the dance floor which has tables around it. On the left-hand side is the stage, where there is room for the band and strippers. The whole room opens onto the sea and has a terrace built on stilts over the water. Pim thought that the air must be much better for the skin and lungs than in Udon, but she was sorry to lose her regular customers and safe income from the show. Still, she had managed to beat heavy competition here to perform three dances a night, and that pushed up her market price considerably. She could ask seven to eight hundred baht for a night, which was two-thirds higher than the normal price in Pattaya.

"You know, you've really got to see things differently here. You're left totally on your own. Sure there are girls who are "married" to pimps or are kept like in a barracks, but most of them are out on their own. They rent their own bungalow and the Syndicate just asks for its cut. For the ones who work the small bars and discos it's just like in Udon. But the punters are a problem. If a warship hasn't just come in, or if there aren't guys out for a weekend lay from Bangkok, then it's nearly all tourists from Europe, America, Australia, Japan or Arab countries. The Japanese and Arabs are OK, because you know where you are with them. They're always drunk and randy and just want to get their end away. They treat the girls like dirt, just like the Thai men do. But the others! They want to have every little bit of you, they want to save you from your fate. They sit there in the *barbos* on the terrace, gawping at the sea and then into your eyes, and talk about love. They believe in it for as long as the holiday mood lasts. You can't get away from them. They want you twenty-four hours a day. They like to think you're their little girlfriend from the

103

tropics. They want to hold your hand and all that crap. And it really gets on your nerves, even if the guy's actually quite nice and good-looking. But all the romantic rubbish makes you money, not just the basic, but presents and tips on top. Some of them apparently even send you money after they've gone home, so that their little darling won't get into anybody else's hands. I'll expect that when I see it! I really want to see you. Come when you can, and bring your *tirak* along."

On Friday afternoon I was sitting with Benjamin in a rattling air-conditioned bus on the way to Pattaya, chewing wind-dried cuttlefish. When we arrived we rented a bungalow chalet at the end of the resort, just behind the Tiffany gay bar. Our wooden chalet could only be reached by a narrow path which was washed at by the high tide. Bare rock came up into the bathroom which was built onto the house like a swallow's nest. We had a terrace looking out onto the sea.

We had arranged to meet Pim at the Fantasy bar at about eight o'clock. That meant we had about half an hour in which to stroll there. The seafood restaurants were filling up, and the first girls were taking their places at the bars. The day shift had come to an end, and there were no more wall-hangings and drinks being sold on the promenade; no more ponies, boats, motorbikes, motorboats and water-skis were being rented out. Benjamin was ogled by some transvestites, who were acting in a particularly tarty way.

"I'll give you this evening off," I said. "Go and get yourself a *gatoy!*"

He laughed and slapped me on the bottom. I was so excited about seeing Pim. I undid another two buttons on my blouse, swung my hips a little more and put my arm around Benjamin's waist. I skipped through the glitter of Pattaya like a prostitute showing off her handsome pimp. I think Benjamin liked this touch of corruption, because there was an extra gleam in his eye.

Pim and I were overjoyed to see each other. That evening I

had my sister and my husband with me, like a real little family. We sat down at a table and ordered a bottle of Mekhong whisky and some of our strong-tasting soda water. We were going to have fun.

Pim liked Benjamin. I could tell that from the little looks she kept giving me. I was proud of him, a gentle, strong and handsome man who could also speak such good Thai. Pim even flirted with him, which I did not mind at all, because it showed that she approved my choice.

Then she had to go on stage. She was as supple as ever, and you could feel the temperature rise in the club. I leaned over in the darkness to Benjamin and whispered wickedly in his ear.

"Don't you like her body? Isn't she sexy? She likes you. I can tell. Would you like to spend the night between her legs? You can have her from me. She is like my sister, and I know her body as well as my own."

He moved closer to me, and I felt his hand moving gently but purposefully towards my crotch, sliding between my thighs and caressing me. His words reached me on his breath.

"You. Only you!"

Pim was not taking any customers that night, so we had the evening to ourselves, just the three of us. When she had finished her last performance we headed with a wonderful sense of relief for the Barbos Restaurant, having first emptied our bottle of whisky. We sat down on a terrace overlooking the sea, and with the gentle night breeze playing around us we devoured the contents of a huge porcelain dish full of sweet and sour fish. Benjamin suggested another strong cocktail to help the digestion, so we descended on a neighbouring bar, where I insisted that the two of them kiss each other and call each other by their childish nicknames.

When the bar shut we were not in the mood for bed. We took off our shoes and ran down to the sea. The sand cushioned our tired feet, and we ran back and forth as the water splashed around our ankles.

105

As dawn broke we saw a fishing boat going out to sea. We called out, jumped up and down and waved a cloth, until the fisherman began to make his way towards us. We began to run to him, but as the water became deeper we could hardly move any more. I haggled with the fishermen, and eventually we climbed into his boat. He took us to the island of Si Chang, where he set us down and went off to his day's work.

We were as playful as puppies, pushing each other and throwing wet sand around. I dug a big hole, saying I was looking for turtles' eggs for my family's breakfast. We had cast aside all restraint, had broken through the barrier between one day and the next. Our freedom of spirit had been brought to life by alcohol, and there was not the least physical coyness left in us. The rising sun tickled the tips of our noses. We tore off our clothes and ran into the sea. When Benjamin stumbled, Pim and I threw ourselves on top of him. He was now on his back and the water was washing around his body. His arms and legs were stretched out. Springing out of the water like a mooring-post was the classically-beautiful, streamlined form of his large, stiff phallus.

I knelt down between his thighs and pulled Pim down. She slid in beneath his arm and pressed her body sideways against his. I put my arm round the back of his neck so that I could stroke Pim's face. My sheath swallowed his blade and they pressed tightly, but smoothly together. My left hand searched for the grotto of Pim's mount of Venus. My tongue explored first Pim's mouth, then Benjamin's. We began to seethe like the spray of a storm in the vent of a volcano, caught up in the ecstasy of sheer sexual freedom, experiencing a complete honesty and equality. We were floating in another world, one filled with joy and harmony.

As the rising sun warmed our bodies we at last became sleepy. We huddled up together in the shade of the palm trees and our breathing became lost in the monotonous beating of the waves.

A *Tiger growling inside*

We went back to Pattaya in the late afternoon on a pleasure boat. Our skin, hair and clothes were crusted with salt and full of sand. Everyone looked at us as if we were survivors from a shipwreck.

On the journey home to Bangkok my mood was pleasantly poised between what I had experienced that weekend and anticipation of my busy week in the city.

I had been able to read and write Latin script with ease for some time now. My success at learning English just increased my impatience.

One evening Benjamin took me to a German restaurant, the Alt Heidelberg in Nanatai Street. For the first time in my life I ate soup with liver dumplings and roast pork in the German style. If you put plenty of seasoning on the food, it did not taste so bad, though I was rather surprised that the kitchens did not cut the food up into bite-size pieces before bringing it to the customer.

Then Benjamin cleared his throat a little self-consciously and asked me if I wanted to learn German now too. I saw the expectation in his eyes and was flattered by his confidence in me. The very next day I signed on at the Goethe Institute for a language course. I was happy to think that I had something of a head start in learning German, since I had already surmounted the problems of a new alphabet and the multisyllable structure of western languages. And what was more, Benjamin was a very patient coach who always found clever ways of helping me to remember things.

My learning was not just confined to languages either. Looking through Benjamin's books and having discussions with him made my questions, which were once so naive and indeterminate, much more clearly defined and to the point. Why should there be so much poverty and social inequality in a country like Thailand which has always had so many riches? Why do the *farangs* have an affluent lifestyle although they do not seem to be more civilised or disciplined than the Thais?

107

How can we preserve our traditional culture while also becoming a technologically developed country? And one question which was especially close to my heart: how can a society
with high Buddhist morals allow, or even *make* women, who
are sometimes little more than children, carry the greatest
burden? The politicians make eloquent speeches, but like
Prapat, the former dictator, they probably have interests in
chains of brothels. The governors of provinces initiate agri-
cultural development schemes, and watch while someone like
Intha, the head of the Thai farmers' union, is shot down with a
price of two hundred baht on his head. And they let the police
take protection money from prostitutes, reducing the income of women who, as it is, have been most severely affected
by the poverty of the farmers.

I had always been a very faithful Buddhist, like all the other
prostitutes. But doubt had secretly set in. What sort of religious morality cruelly allows young girls to be forced into
prostitution by poverty, and then views these same girls with
moral outrage, punishing them with the threat of reincarnation
in an unworthy form? They are left to the worst fate of all, the
wretchedness of utter self contempt.

I began to study books on Buddhism. Benjamin was a
member of the Siam Society, and I found its library, set in a
lovely garden in the Soi Asok, to be a haven of peace in the city.
There was also the replica of a northern farmstead there, and I
would often sit in its shade and read without any disturbance. I
also often went to the D.K. bookshop in Siam Square. I had
heard that the shop had played an important role in the
democratic movement before the downfall of the dictators
Thanom and Prapat, since it had been a centre of intellectual
resistance. I found a fascinating book there, Chit Pumisak's
history of Thailand.

Chit was an historian and man of letters. He was also a poet,
and had dedicated a poem to my homeland in the north-east,
the Isan.

A Tiger growling inside

"The sky holds no water;
Worse still, the earth is just sand
Which swallows the endless tears.
Our blood trickles away in this parched land.
Our arms and shoulders are strong,
And everyone can hear the agitation in our voices.
Man of the Isan, rise up and use
your strong arms to fight to the end!
When the dry winds whine and moan,
and the border between woodland and field
  becomes ever more blurred,
Then our people arise in their thousands.
Who would dare to destroy us all?"

Chit joined the guerillas and was shot in 1965 in the Puphan mountains in the north-east.

I had only known history in terms of the individual stories of kings, generals and bonzes, but Chit always tried to seek out the contribution of the ordinary people to the course of history.

In the past Buddhist monasteries had played a large part in the education and social life of the people, but in times of trouble seem rarely to have taken the people's side.

I began to see that Buddhism was a religion with dual standards. In our culture there is the contradiction that the women are the essential social force in rural life while in religious life they are expected to take an obedient and self-effacing role. Buddhism began in India, and took from Hinduism the idea of woman as a frightening and mysterious entity. Only men are considered capable of raising themselves from the physical to the spiritual. Women are fated to remain as earth-mothers, with an almost animal physicality. Manu, the law-giver of ancient India warned learned men against women, who could make them into slaves of desire and emotion. He was also the originator of

109

the double image of woman as both saint and whore:

"No man should be in a lonely place with his mother, sister or daughter, for the senses are mighty and can overpower even a wise man!"

What explosive undercurrents are at work in his suppressed and neurotic incestual desires for his "sacred" and taboo-laden female relatives.

A fourteenth-century Thai cosmography places women in the lower order of living beings. Above are enthroned the Brahman divinities, who are all male. Even women becoming *mae chi*, or nuns, occupy a lowly position in the Buddhist hierarchy. But behind this formal system lurks a deep fear of everything feminine. King Mongkut, who was a monk for twenty-seven years before coming to the throne, put it about that monks could be seduced and driven to madness by women. Purity and enlightenment were the "masculine" principles, sensuality and madness the "feminine" ones. The mortally dangerous female had to be confined within a cage of prohibitions and codes of behaviour, and traditional literature is full of moral doctrine for women.

The most famous figure in traditional literature is Sida (Sita), heroine of the Ramakien (Ramayana). The bride of Phra Ram (Rama), she is abducted by an evil fiend. She is eventually freed after a violent battle, but has to undergo a trial of fire in order to prove her chastity. She passes through the trial, but male fantasies can grant her no peace. Once again there is suspicion that she did not remain pure during her captivity. When she gives birth to two children in exile the gods take pity and intercede for her.

Isn't Sida's fate like the life of a prostitute? Although she is supposed to have remained chaste while in the monster's power, the men still neurotically imagine the wanton sign of the whore to be hanging over her. She is doomed to be both saint and whore simultaneously.

Contempt for whores is a male gesture of protection which

is both defiant and aggressive, since in her loins the whore holds danger and sorcery. The saint is a whore, and the whore is a saint; mother, sister and daughter are all temptresses, yet also symbols of sacred purity. This crazy confusion of perception can only lead to fear, and men therefore try to protect themselves from "contamination" by anything feminine. Thus women's clothes should not be washed with men's, otherwise the men in question will lose their spiritual strength or sexual potency.

Men, inherently weaker and more prone to anxiety, are meant to be spiritually superior to women, but cannot free themselves from the curse of the evil deed. Feminine sensuality finds revenge for its condemnation. Wild, poisonous and magical sexual fantasies finding their way into the blood may be temporarily suppressed, only to rise again from the darkness with even greater supernatural power. Men fear the vengeance of jealous women. A deceived wife could secretly mix vaginal secretions into her husband's food and thus suspend the protective power of amulets and tattoos. It is said that we whores sprinkle water mixed with vaginal fluids around our homes in order to create an irresistible attraction for customers. Menstrual blood is something filthy, and men should not therefore have sex with a woman during her period, as newly-married couples are often told.

The behaviour prescribed for women during lovemaking reflects masculine fears: women should be physically submissive, passive and devoted; they are not to be made aware of their almost limitless capacity for orgasm. Men's sexual persecution complex leads them to try and protect their potency with magical symbols, while women are denied any symbols of this kind. The power of the sorceress in the loins of the woman and whore obviously provokes a great deal of fear . . .

★

I had just bought some books for reading practice in the Chalermnit bookshop in the Erawan arcade which specialises in German literature.

I hailed a taxi. I leaned down to the passenger window to tell the driver where to go and to agree the fare.

The driver turned to me. I saw a nervous twitch of the eyes, an emaciated face with a growth of stubble and a patina on the skin from sweat and the smog-laden air. Suddenly my heart skipped a beat. It was Lek! The gentle boy I had loved in the bamboo grove. It was only when I spoke that he recognised me. I sat down next to him, my knees weak. The hooters of the cars behind made it clear that we were blocking the road. Lek would have to get going, so we joined the stream of traffic. It made me so unhappy to see his eyes obscured every few moments by his twitch.

"Lek, why aren't you at home?"

He swallowed. "I need some extra cash. I'm going back for the harvest. All being well it'll be a good one. I'm not coming back next year to the town. Life's tough here. I sometimes don't even get enough to pay for the rent on my taxi and the petrol."

I felt helpless. All I could find to say to him was:

"Are you hungry?"

He did not answer me, but I asked him to turn left into the next *soi*, where there was a little restaurant. He ate ravenously. I ordered a large bottle of beer which I hoped would calm him down.

"Don't work any more today," I said. I did not want to hurt him, and as I slipped a thousand baht into his hand I said, "Things are going well for me, and after all, I look on you as a brother." He obviously needed some help, and I was reacting instinctively. I could see he was relieved, but there was an expression of sadness and shame in his eyes. We still cared for each other like brother and sister. That was all that remained of our idyllic love.

112

I plucked up courage to ask him about my family, and was overjoyed with his answer.

"Oh, all is well with them. Your money has solved all their problems. The buffalo are strong and healthy, and your people have been able to buy another five *rai* of paddyfields. And your big brother Thongbai is back home. The only thing they worry about is you. They've no idea what has happened to you. What shall I tell them?"

He obviously wanted to know too. I looked at him and touched his hand for a moment.

"It hasn't been easy for me either. It's been a struggle, but I've made a lot of money. I'm not an innocent little peasant girl any more. I'm a *farang*'s woman now." He looked so downcast that I wanted to take him in my arms and comfort him. "How wonderful it could have been for us. We would have told our children stories in the evening while the rain fell outside and we would have enjoyed the festivals at the temple. But we're outcasts. For thousands of years our forefathers lived as we wanted to, but we have been exiled from that existence. I hope you'll find your way back home, Lek. And don't worry about me. Tell my parents I'm marrying the *farang* and going back to his country with him. I'll write to you all."

I had arranged to meet Benjamin not far away, and went there on foot. I felt sad after I had said goodbye to Lek. It was strange to look at him and to think that he could have been the father of my children. Then he drove off in his taxi. I hoped so much that he could be a farmer again and would not have to leave our village. Perhaps one of my younger sisters would fall in love with him.

I told Benjamin what had happened. We did not say much that evening. I was thankful to him for being understanding and staying away from me. That made me feel even closer to him.

★

The year was marching on. I was so caught up in my study that Benjamin decided I should take a few days' holiday.

We took a sleeper to Chiang Mai, and stayed there just long enough to see the Doi Suthep with its mountain monastery overlooking the Chiang Mai valley. Then we hired two Japanese 500 c.c. cross-country bikes and set off northwards into the mountains.

Benjamin knew some people working on a project in the Samoeng district. We got to the isolated valley just before dark. We had lost our way earlier and had ended up having to cross rivers and climb steep mountain paths. We spent the night in the project office, left our bikes there the next day and set off with our rucksacks for the mountain jungle. We wanted to be alone, so we kept away from the tribal villages. For several days we made our way through the shady green cathedral of the jungle with the sounds of animals' voices instead of organ music.

We got our timing wrong one day. It was getting gloomy and beginning to pour with rain. The red earth of the sloping path became slippery and dangerous. We carried on for a little until we noticed a charred smell, and were relieved when we came to a clearing that had been burned in the jungle. This could only mean that a village was near, and sure enough we reached one after crossing another path.

The village elder granted us hospitality, and in the evening we were invited to smoke a pipe of opium. The old social order was obviously still retained here. Young working people were not expected to smoke on a regular basis, since opium was a privilege of the old men with their long beards, who, after working all their lives were able to heighten their wealth of experience with insights into a raised consciousness.

The rain splashed against the leaves above us, and swathes of mist floated spectrally between the posts of the houses, winding themselves high up around the trees and searching every nook and cranny of the valley. We had wrapped ourselves in blankets and were looking down at the vista from the porch. The village elder had taken his leave and had made his slow way into the darkness inside the hut. The tops of our heads felt as if they had opened up, and streams of ethereal airiness were flowing in. Then we too went inside to curl up beneath the blankets.

I do not know whether I was naked or not, and I cannot be sure that Benjamin was inside me, but I was floating in a world of erotic fantasy which was bringing me to constant shudders of ecstasy. His skin was like damp velvet to the touch.

The trembling lips of my womb opened to him and stroked the swollen blue veins of his spout as he drained away in me, feeding me back the nectar with his mouth. Our glittering astral bodies spun through the endless spaces of the night. When he kissed me our lips froze into one, and when he ejaculated inside me I felt burning cold waves of liquid helium in my belly. One vividly clear image after another flowed through my mind. Finally the vortex in my head, spinning as smoothly as a potter's wheel, slowly released me from its pull and I flew away as light as a feather.

I woke up in Benjamin's arms, my mind absolutely clear.

We crossed the mountain heights and went back to the Samoeng valley. We spurred our bikes on to get back in time to catch the train home to Bangkok.

★

Time was inexorably passing. I felt tension rising within me, I was getting out of pace. The hourglass was gently and ceaselessly trickling away, and driving me to desperation. All my cool resolve and clear intentions were dissolving into secret tears.

I got a shock when I realised that I had forgotten my pill

115

three days running – fortunately it was just before my period. My feelings would not be ruled by my head, and as time ran out for both of us our feelings were becoming irresistibly stronger.

I tried to get myself back on an even keel, and went to the gynaecologist. I had been wanting to come off the pill for a long time because I was inherently mistrustful of chemical methods. I thought the coil would be a better idea for me, since it would put up a literal barrier inside me, but it did nothing to assuage my longings.

I tried hammering the message home to myself:

"You are a whore with a contract for a specified time. You have no right to break up a marriage based on harmony and friendship, one with children who need to be protected, just because you have silly romantic dreams. You are a whore, you are young, pretty, free and proud, and you have everything going for you."

But nothing helped. What I needed was shock therapy. I took the first bus to Pattaya without leaving a message for Benjamin. I cried my eyes out in Pim's arms. Then I made up my mind that I was going to make a pick-up that night. It was the only way to bring myself back down to earth.

Pim could do nothing to stop me. I borrowed her sexiest clothes, and splashed my eyes with cold water to stop them from looking red and tear-swollen.

Because she danced there Pim did not need to buy drink vouchers at the Fantasy Club. She wanted to sneak me past the doorman, but I insisted on buying my ticket like a good whore. It was only professional, and I was trying to calm myself down with the discipline of work. Once at the bar I sat like a cashier counting how many men were taking a look at me. The till was ringing away.

I was on special offer and would take the first that came along.

"Have you got anything on this evening?"

"No." Good, a cool voice, quick to choose and quick to get to work. Was his accent Danish, German, French, Dutch or Arabic? *Mai pen arai*, so what? In the hotel room I would probably have to pull his foreskin back and fondle his penis. When he came I would ungraciously take the money and go. If not, *mai pen arai*.

As Pim danced his eyes cruelly devoured her. I hissed as he began to grope inside my panties in the dark. He took the hint, but I knew he was just doing it to build up his excitement. He tried to make up by putting his arm around me. Suddenly I felt his body go tense. I turned round to look at him. His eyes were starting from his head. His face was contorted with pain, the veins in his temples were full to bursting. Behind him was Benjamin, squeezing the guy's jugular between the fingers of his right hand! He leaned down and spat the words "No scandal" at him, then pulled me up with his left arm. I followed him, not knowing what to think. I was surprised, I could not believe what had happened, but I could feel a great rush of joy. Pim saw us from the stage. She stopped for a moment, took the situation in with her wide eyes, and carried on dancing with a little smile on her lips.

We were standing at the same spot on the shore where we had seen the fishing boat. We were holding each other, both in tears, our lips burning with the salty taste. He was speaking to me with his body. I wanted to hear the message, but at the same time it hurt me.

"You must stay by my side forever!"

We were like a suicidal pair of Japanese lovers on the snow-covered heights of Mount Fujiyama, looking down into the depths of the crater. Our feelings could not take us any further. There was only one, cruel solution – to throw ourselves into the volcano, into the fiery bowels of the earth.

The sea breeze could not pass between our bodies. The night dew surrounded us, sealing our togetherness. But these natural forces also cooled my thoughts.

117

My feelings had reached their highest peak. It was time to go slowly back down to valleys and the rice fields, where life was simple, but where there was a quiet understanding of the constraints of reality and a self-denying recognition of the ethic of survival and resourcefulness.

★

My course at the Goethe Institute had just finished and Benjamin had saved up some holiday, so we decided to go south to the tip of Thailand's geographical elephant's trunk. We finally crossed the two-hundred-metre-long bridge over the Andanam Sea to the island of Phuket. We could see the winding shafts of the tin mines in the distance, like rollercoasters of bamboo. I suddenly thought how gibbons would have a wonderful time swinging about there. We went to the west coast of the island and rented a bungalow in a new development which was surrounded by luxuriant vegetation on the banks of a stream running down to the sea. But we were only intending to leave our things there.

We then hired a fishing sampan and tackle, and got hold of a canvas awning, ropes, blankets, cooking equipment and utensils, and a big plastic balloon to hold drinking water. Our little boat was heavily loaded down as it chugged through the archipelago westwards into the Andaman Sea. After several hours we stopped on a small island far out to sea and far away from any other human beings. We were going to spend twelve days on this island, twelve days we would count by cutting notches in a palm tree with a machete. We had left our watches, which also showed the date, back at the bungalow.

We dragged the heavy boat onto the brilliant white sand and tied it to the closest palm, which was about ten metres from the water. We then extended the awning between that tree and five others. The sea breeze caught it immediately and puffed it gently up. We put everything beneath the awning and then buried the water-balloon in the sand, putting it deep enough down for it to be cooled by the natural moisture beneath the surface.

I scraped out a pit for the fire and went to find wood and dried palm leaves to burn. In the process I could explore our own little island, which was about three hundred metres across. All it consisted of was the clump of palm trees with sand all round, and it was only about fifteen metres above sea level at the highest point in the centre.

Benjamin cut down some bamboo, split it and built a raised framework for us to sit and sleep on without being too bothered by the sandfleas.

We were now ready to start living out what was almost a cliché: the primeval dream of two lovers alone on an isolated paradise island. We took off our clothes and spent the whole day naked. Our attraction for each other was inevitable and undisguised.

We tested our bed out and found the creaking and groaning of the bamboo so exciting that it was enough on its own to act as an aphrodisiac. Afterwards I went into the sea and crouched down in the smooth water like some prehistoric amphibian creature. The warmth of the water made the semen gather up in little lumps and the crabs in the sea were treated to a protein-packed delicacy.

Our senses were honed by the whisper of the sea and the gentle breath of the breeze. Our skin soon tanned enough not to soak up too much heat from the sun. Benjamin's stubble began to show, and the bleaching effect of the sun and sea brought out various shades in the hairs; I even found some red and grey. After three days the bristles became soft and did not scratch any more.

In the morning we washed ourselves with the dew that had gathered overnight. But we also liked the little traces of salt on our bodies, since we could lick them off each other, concentrating on the most sensitive points.

We went out fishing when we were in the mood and when we had to add to the supplies we had wrapped up in leaves and buried in the sand.

We were overflowing with energy. We ran coltishly around our island, splashing and diving and wrestling with each other. We always ended up making love. Our senses were so alive, so strong and full of desire, that we just had to look for a moment at each other's tanned and lithe body to be seduced.

I made up a game for us to play. I gathered up pastel-coloured shells and went up to Benjamin with them. "Well then, street stud, how much do you cost? I'll give you five shells if you do what I want." He liked the game, but after a time he began to strike a tough bargain, pushing the price higher so I had to find more and more shell money. He already had a pile of it – for his old age, so he said.

It was like paradise. But then the gods became envious. It was on the evening of our last day, just as we were about to open our one bottle of *Gai-Daeng* whisky as a farewell gesture, that they decided to vent their wrath.

A whirlwind was on the horizon. How much time did we have before it came to us?

Panic triggered off our instincts and we dragged the boat through the trees to the top of the island. We pulled it upright against the trunk of a big palm tree that must have withstood many a storm, and then tied it up as quickly as possible, but we were careful to make it secure, hoping that the floodwater and the rain would not damage it. We were pouring with sweat. When we tried to hold on to each other we just slid apart. All our supplies had been used up, but we rolled everything else up in the sail and tied it together. Benjamin climbed almost to the top of a palm tree and secured the bundle to it. By now the storm was rushing through the trees with the sound of breath being drawn in through clenched teeth. What could we do now? Without saying a word we both knew. We looked around to find the next strongest tree in the clump at the middle of the island. We still had a large sack of waterproof canvas which had lots of loops round it. Benjamin climbed three-quarters of the way up the tree and attached the sack on the side leeward of the storm. He then managed to tie it surprisingly well to the tree by putting strong rope through the loops. Benjamin motioned to me to come up and pointed to the whisky bottle. He helped me climb into the makeshift crow's nest and then got in himself. The sack reached up to my armpits and there was enough room for us to stand in it pressed closely together. Since our arms were still free we wound the rest of the rope several times round the trunk and our bodies. If the tree did not get uprooted, and if we were not drowned by the flood like cats in a sack, we stood some sort of chance.

Then the rain began to beat down. We pressed our faces to the trunk of the tree. Benjamin pulled my face close to his and I could feel his lips forming the word "*Tirak*".

He drew the bottle of whisky out of the sack, and we emptied it, taking long draughts of the fiery liquid. My stomach could hardly take it. The alcohol immediately took effect on our punchdrunk brains. Benjamin roared in a voice loud enough to carry over the storm,

"Genie of the bottle! We're sending you on a journey. Wherever you may be washed up, tell of our love!"

He screwed the top back on the bottle and threw it into the raging waters which by now had reached the highest point of the island below us. The ritual of Benjamin's words brought me a moment of calm in the midst of my turmoil.

We dug our fingernails into the overlapping layers of the tree trunk, not that it would have helped us if the rope gave way.

We had by now reached the limit of our endurance. The rain and spray were driving at us so hard that we could hardly

121

breathe. The water would come up over us soon. The waves were crashing against us with greater and greater force. The trees seemed hardly able to take any more; they were bent almost horizontal. I pressed myself even harder against Benjamin's naked, wet body. I wished I was lying in his embrace at the bottom of the sea. Then I lost consciousness.

How deceptive nature can be. When I came to, the sea still seemed a little rough but it had gone back to its normal level, and showed no sign of the temperament it had displayed the night before. The terrifying black and white of the waves had turned to turquoise for the shallow water and a brilliant blue for the depths.

The sun rose in the sky. Benjamin was still asleep. He must have stayed awake to keep watch over me and then fallen into an exhausted sleep himself. I kissed him, turned his face to the sun and whispered in his ear.

"The night is over. The sun has won the battle." He blinked, and then remembered where he was. Then we both began to laugh until the tears streamed down our cheeks.

"Look! The other trees and the rope didn't give way."

Though our hands were numb and our arms and legs were suffering from cramp we managed to undo the rope and crawl clumsily and stiffly down from our tree. We collapsed onto the white sand and let the sun warm us. There was little we could say, but we knew that together we had been to the limits of human experience.

The outboard motor of the sampan had been wrapped in plastic and was undamaged, so there was nothing to prevent us leaving. This time we had much less to load on the boat. We waded into the water and climbed on board. As we looked back our island became smaller and smaller until it was nothing but a tiny speck on the horizon.

★

A *Tiger growling inside*

There was bad news waiting for me when we got back. My old teacher had suffered a stroke and was now paralysed down one side and confined to bed. I went to visit him often, each time taking new English books from the D.K. shop with me.

Then Benjamin told me he had to spend three weeks visiting projects in various parts of the country. That evening he seemed distracted, hardly able to speak, his eyes unseeing. He slept badly too, sweating heavily and squeezing his body against me as if to hold onto me. When he left I felt I was floating in a void surrounded by ghostly forebodings. I decided to do something concrete to rid myself of this feeling of uncertainty. I went to the bank to transfer twenty thousand baht to my family, then I collected my bank statements which I looked through in the taxi on the way home. I must have gone pale because the driver asked me if he ought to drive more slowly.

One hundred and twenty thousand baht had been transferred to my account. A final payment for my future. The temporary contract had run out.

I needed final proof. I had never been through Benjamin's papers, but now I went to his desk and opened the middle drawer. I saw a pale yellow airline ticket, Bangkok-Frankfurt with a connection to Stuttgart. I did not care what date it was for. Next to it was a photo, dated ten days previously. On it was written. "We are so looking forward to seeing you!" It showed a woman with two lovely blond children. She was attractive, but a little hard-looking. She seemed older than Benjamin.

This picture helped break my fall back down to reality. I might have been broken to pieces otherwise. This family photo showed me everything I did not have. But it also made me feel responsible and generous. I, the whore, could have jeopardised this idyll. Now my feelings were wavering between a confident sense of my magical sexual power and the comforting thought that I still had lots of time and

123

opportunities for finding a love which I could rely on to last. If that was what I wanted.

This did not stop me from feeling sad, but I now began to think of practicalities. It seemed as if I had planned it several times before.

I sent a telegram to Pim, then I packed a case with clothes and books, which I would take in the taxi to Pattaya.

I took a flower and put it on Benjamin's desk. It would be withered by the time he got back.

What message should I leave him?

He had explained to me the significance of the seasons in his country, and, being sentimental, I left this poem next to the flower.

> *"It was a spring*
> *that never came,*
> *and never turned to summer.*
> *But it is still alive.*
> *Because I had the humanity*
> *to learn that*
> *what I possessed*
> *dies in the autumn,*
> *and remains*
> *what I never had*
> *and only longed for*
> *in winter."*

A few tears dropped onto the paper. Damn.

Limbo

Life in Pattaya

Pim's feelings wavered between happiness at seeing me again and fear that being apart from Benjamin would trouble me for a long time to come. But she was reassured to see that I was firmly back in the swing of things. I was not complaining, bemoaning my fate or getting lost in tearful memories. I did not even allow myself to have a Blue Monday off to let myself nurse a hangover.

The same evening that I arrived in Pattaya I was back onstage with Pim. After a year away from each other we were back together again, the Siamese Sisters. I had moved into Pim's bungalow which stood in a peaceful spot – though not far away from Pattaya's "Sin Mile".

★

Before the American intervention in Indochina, Pattaya was a sleepy fishing village and health resort in the shadow of Hua Hin. But during the Vietnam War it exploded to become the biggest brothel in Southeast Asia after Saigon and Bangkok.

125

The US Rest and Recreation Program dumped planeload after planeload of soldiers there, and warships sent waves of landing-craft to the beach, which until then had only been busy at weekends. The place was flooded by sex-hungry men. A sort of lunar cycle developed. The floodwaters subsided, only to come crashing back, drawing hordes of girls from the inland regions to Pattaya. The young peasant girls were virtually crushed beneath the huge and drunken bodies of the napalm bombers, the My-Lai murderers, the backroom boys and the junkies who just couldn't take the fighting. The female youth of the poor was being literally bought up as soon as they reached adolescence. And how things changed from one night to the next for these girls. There would be one punter tired of the war and full of frustration who would just want to share a joint and coyly hold hands. Then there would be a hardened soldier from the front line who would tear a girl's arse open as if he were shoving a bayonet into a Vietcong. It was all a terrible clash of sexes, races and cultures.

Then came the calm after the storm. The puffed-up cockerels of America had turned out to be capons. The battlefields became rice-fields again. But what was to become of the camp-followers who were now suffering from a lack of customers?

A new market for Pattaya opened up at just the right time. Mass tourism in the tropics was a growth area, the pitiful remains of the fundamental human drive for exploration. The tourist in the tropics makes no effort to get to know foreign cultures or languages. Well, there is a bit of culture – a couple of hours of Thai folk music and dance one evening, and they can get all the traditional civilisation over in one go by taking a day-trip to the "ancient city" in Samut Prakan where there is an open-air museum with life-size reconstructions of sixty-five of the country's most impressive monuments. And what else? A clean, pretty luxurious hotel with air-conditioning, a German manager, a Swiss chef (with steaks flown in from

New Zealand), a private beach and the hotel's own Maritime Club. Although the hotel does not exactly welcome female overnight guests in the rooms, they are tolerated for a supplementary payment of one hundred baht.

"Oh, and it's not far to the Fantasy Club. *Honi soit qui mal y pense.* You might as well have gone to Spain otherwise. And everyone's really earned his holiday, from a workman from Wanne-Eickel to a lawyer from Munich. And when you're on holiday it just doesn't matter about your background. You see each other at the Fantasy, you're wearing the same sort of Bermudas and the same shirts with the pattern of palm trees. Your holiday sweethearts may even know each other well. After your third *mai tai* cocktail by the swimming pool, you might even consider taking a *gatoy* up to your room – know what I mean? A really pretty little 'girl' with a squeaky voice. But they're probably thieving little bastards, and likely as not you'll catch something from them.

"And have you eaten Thai food? Bloody hot it is, I can tell you. But you have to go to their restaurants or the girls sulk. They've got to have their rice, it's sacred to them. My little bird, for example, you can go for a proper European meal with her, but she pokes her food around on the plate in such a way, and she holds the knife all wrong, and you think that she'll have to have her bowl of rice otherwise she's going to lose weight. And I wouldn't like that. She's really got it all in the right places. A gorgeous little arse that waggles about like a plate of blancmange. And her tits are like two lovely little Matterhorns. And, between you and me, no other women in the world have got pussies like the Thai ones. Hardly any hair at all. Like little watermelons, all red and juicy inside.

"Is this your first time here? Then let me tell you something as an old hand. Don't change girls too often. Find yourself a nice little holiday sweetheart who's got what it takes. Sure, there's something to be said for having a different one every night, but you really run the risk of getting your fingers – or something else – burned. And I can tell you, nothing's sadder than having to sit drinking mineral water in Pattaya and watch all the goings-on. And have you ever tried peeing with the clap? You'd think your thing was exploding, it hurts so much. And that's your holiday up the spout for the year. I've had this one twice before. She waits for me all year. I send her something every now and then for her kid. But let's not pretend I don't know she has other men. But if I wanted to marry her, I bet she'd say yes. What they really want is to come over to Germany, they want to have their slice of the cake too. Affluent society and all that. I'm a widower, you know, my wife died young, breast cancer. Of course I've often wondered whether I should take her home with me. And don't think that I've got anything against their people. If you want to see what they can do, just look at the Japs. They're clever monkeys – I mean that in the nicest way, of course. And all the Women's Lib stuff back home can really turn you off a girl. I'd do anything for a good German woman, as long as she made me feel that she admires me as a man, well, not exactly admire me perhaps, but, you know what I mean, that she really sees something in me. Some hope! You'd be lucky these days. You work for them, you even hoover the carpet for them, and they still scream at you. When I think about my little darling here! When she smiles at me with her eyes looking down like that, it warms the cockles of my heart. And she will insist on doing my washing for me, even though there's an express laundry at the hotel. I pay her for it, of course. But there's more to it than that. There's something romantic about it all. That's the sort of attitude a woman ought to have to a man. And how about in bed! You'll have found out a bit about that already, I expect. All you ever hear back home is, 'Don't snore so loud. I'm tired. We only did it the day before yesterday. The bed squeaks. What will the neighbours think? It's my period. You've been drinking again. You're hurting me!' And when she does feel like it, you get told

128

off for it being over too quickly. It stops you from feeling like you're a real man. But it's different here in Thailand. Here you're still treated like a man. You know, sometimes it's like I'm in seventh heaven. I lie there in the bath, she soaps me up, washes me off, dries me. I lie there on the bed and she massages me. Have you tried body-to-body massage yet? No? Then you should ask for it, it's all part of the service. When she rubs her firm little tits all over you, it's just too much. That stops John from being a dull boy. And their skin, so firm and smooth, and their hair, all long and silky. They're still the way God meant them to be. And those slanty eyes. I always call mine my little Siamese cat. It was the eyes that did it. They really turn me on. The secrets of the orient are behind there. It's not like some watery-eyed old fish looking at you. There's real magic in their eyes . . . But where were we? Oh yes, marrying them. You know it's one thing looking forward to your dream holiday all year, but getting married? Your routine would put an end to the romance. And no matter how much you love each other, there's a big difference between your ways of life, and you never know if the girl will ever be able to get used to it. And all these Thai women are crazy about kids. They want a whole litter of them. You know, no one could ever call me a racist, but I wouldn't want my kids to have slanty eyes. And have you ever seen that sly look the orientals give you? They don't get angry, they just look at you. No, I'd rather slog all year so I can have my six weeks in . . . What's this place called again? . . . Yeah, Nirvana, that's it."

*

As Pim had suggested in her first letter the main problem in our work was the romantic expectations of the clients. In

Udon my work hours had been clearly defined. Erotic dance was my special skill, and I would spend half the night with clients I had chosen. But the days were mine to do with as I wished. In Pattaya it was not possible to have an organised timetable. There were simply not the facilities at the Fantasy Club to mount a show with a carefully rehearsed fixed prog- ramme, and so our show there was just a pale reflection of the one we had presented in Udon. Of course, our role as dancers gave us an advantage over the other girls, but we were not able to get so carried away as we titillated the audience, and so the punters were not as ready as they had been to pay almost any price for us. Pim had given me lots of advice, but I still had numerous bad experiences with clients before I became more canny and found my own particular style.

I discovered that it was mostly the Arabs, Japanese and other orientals who were interested in just spending the night with a girl. They did not have any romantic fantasies, which meant that I could have the days to myself. Yet I decided not to take on any more of these customers, because I found them to be both stingy and crude. To them you are just some kind of sexual slot machine which is expected to deliver the goods within a certain time in return for the money put in. And your performance is never reflected in what they pay you, since their all-in price is supposed to include anything from the missionary position to fellatio to anal intercourse and so on. I sometimes left tricks of this kind having been physically maltreated. It was like spending the whole night being raped, and I was ready to put up a lot of resistance. But when I got back to the bungalow the next morning I felt broken, sore, weary, and heavy-headed. I wanted to be sick, and there was deep anger emanating from my sore vagina.

I soon learned to assess the punters, to pick and choose and only allow entry to certain applicants. I limited my clientele to Europeans, Americans, Australians and New Zealanders – the "romantics". I was soon able to weed out by instinct the pimps looking for new employees, the sex maniacs, the loudmouthed drunks and the calculating perverts.

I could afford to be more choosy than most of the other girls. My bank account gave me confidence and a certain independence. And by making myself into something special I did not lose out. In fact, it was the pushy girls who failed to make pick-ups, since the punters like to feel that they have "conquered" a girl. The less approachable she is, the "purer" she appears to be, so making herself worthy to receive avowals of love.

During the monsoons there are far fewer tourists in Pattaya, so the place is overstaffed with girls. Life is expensive there, a lot of money has to go on clothes, and since many of the girls are careless with their money the competition for business becomes especially strong. It is of course the older and less attractive women who are most badly hit, especially if they have not put any money away, which is all too often the case. It shocks me to see so many women who have been on the game for a dozen years or so, working for themselves, and have no savings to show for it. It seems so obvious to take advantage of the relatively high income you enjoy during your prime years as a whore for the foreigners, when you are still young, and build up some reserves of cash. I was often teased for being thrifty, but I could not understand the foolishness of women who brushed all their cares aside by saying they would end up marrying a *farang* one day, and so not have to worry any more. So my bank account just kept on growing, even though I occasionally transferred money to my family. I would have become frustrated and embittered if I had been selling my young and beautiful body just to have a hand-to-mouth existence. I tolerated life as a prostitute because I was aiming for financial independence, and I wanted to have achieved it long before my looks began to fade.

The "romantic" customers demanded an awful lot of you. They were also the ones most ready to hand out a lot of money, so that was another reason why I specialised in them. What was more, most of them were not even especially demanding as far as sex was concerned. In fact, since the "romances" often lasted several weeks, an almost marital routine developed: once before going to sleep, finishing off with a good-night kiss, and perhaps once more on waking up to work off the morning erection. Of course some of them had a higher sex drive than others, while some of them hardly ever seemed to get excited. I developed an eye for the sort of punter who, once you had weighed up all the pros and cons, was the least hard work and also the most profitable. He had to be physically appealing, well cared-for, in good physical shape and clean. That way these intense relationships were at least not totally without any aesthetic appeal. If I found a man to be good-looking and fastidious in his habits, then intimate contact with him was much more tolerable. If he was also gentle and fairly self-contained, for instance if he liked reading, then being together with him twenty-four hours a day was not too much of a strain for me. With the help of my instincts and a little luck I generally managed to find punters with a little elegance and style who managed to reduce the strain of a relationship based on commercial values. The holidaymaker was of course also helped by the corny soft-focus imagery of love in a tropical paradise.

My looks, my youth, my sexual promise, my subtlety, and not least my knowledge of languages soon made me a name among the barmen and night porters at expensive hotels like the Regent Pattaya and the Royal Cliff, who would then recommend me quietly to the more discerning lone traveller. I found more and more that I was attending discreetly arranged rendezvous in the coffee shops, restaurants and nightclubs of the hotels. I was having less and less to do with the crowds of drunken lads on a package holiday at the Nipa Lodge.

I only knew one other girl in Pattaya who could speak and write a western language. She had been a teacher in Hua Hin and now worked behind the bar in Die Zwei, which was run by two German women. But she was not able to take such profitable advantage of her linguistic ability.

She was trapped with "the boys" who spent their time at the bar where she worked, at the German restaurant attached to it, or at the Fantasy Club. I thought that if you were going to have a tropical romance, then you might as well make a little effort. The holiday mood and the sexy atmosphere cannot get you through those inevitable dull patches which occur when you cannot communicate with each other in a language you both understand, and the girls in Pattaya could only manage the mixed-up pidgin which had developed there. A few of them had bilingual pocket dictionaries which they could use to point out a word to help the elementary conversation along. My intention was to stimulate the generosity of my romantically-minded punters as much as possible, and this was only possible if you really made them fall in love with you. And it was more than just a sexual bond, you had to become "soul mates" through really talking to each other. Now I was able to use the knowledge of language and other things that I had acquired during my time with Benjamin. My languages could also be used to exploit the customers' feelings in the longer term. In Pattaya there were several failed Thai academics who were parasites on the prostitutes. They were paid by the girls to write "love letters" to the punters in their own countries. When business was bad these letters brought them in a lot of money. But the ghost letterwriters did not provide very good work. They catalogued the sender's woes without adding any touches of imagination: "I love you. I cannot sleep without you. I only want to be with you. But I have to go to bed with other men so that I can live." Then they just put the number of the girl's bank account straight down on the paper. These standard letters soon chilled even the most ardent lover, making him suspicious in the process.

I could write in English and German, and was able to

produce much more credible letters written with the personal touch. Over my time in Pattaya I built up a long list of correspondents in places ranging from Australia to Norway, but there were more in Germany than anywhere else. I began to make more money from writing letters than from soliciting. I took fewer and fewer customers, so gaining more time for myself, which I could spend thinking and reading. I needed to cut down on the number of punters, because not only did I have to polish up my writing technique, but I also had lots of regular clients who came back again and again to Pattaya for their holidays, sometimes twice a year. I had to be careful not to get double booked!

I also really sharpened up my acting skills in Pattaya. I had created erotic illusions when I danced in Udon, but here I was unable to put myself out of reach on a stage. And I was having to provide a different sort of sexual service, since you were expected to stay close to your client for quite a long time at a stretch. I was able to keep some sort of freedom by choosing my men carefully, but the fundamental problem was that I was being bought up wholesale for an uninterrupted period. And I still had to give my customers at least the illusion of romance, which meant that I could never give the game away at all: there could be no tension in my vagina, he was not to see me yawning, my mouth could not be seen to turn down at the corners, my eyes could not narrow, I was not to look uninterested. I learned the ultimate technique of the prostitute: I had to play at being in love. I was following in the footsteps of the hetaera, the *cocotte*, the geisha, the mistress – and many a housewife.

Not that I had any pangs of conscience or doubts about my principles in behaving the way I did. Why should I have had any? I was not setting out to get a man attached to me, to get myself married off to him and so buy myself a comfortable way of life. I may have expected payment for what I was doing. But it was fun for the man. He could enjoy himself without having to feel guilty about it, he was not making any commitments. And I was not going to blackmail him with moral reproaches, pregnancies or suicide threats. I was being quite honest about it. After all, when you buy a ticket for the theatre you know that you are going to see a play. I can't help it if members of the audience go backstage afterwards and knock at the actresses' dressing-rooms, obsessed with the idea of turning dream into reality.

But my most effective method was my letters. The punters would have been back in their everyday routine for a long time, yet the exotic poisoned arrows would still strike them to the heart. I was never emphatic in my letters, I did not turn on the sentiment or make hollow promises. But my letters were full of allure. I talked about little things that had happened, I described the weather, mentioned people we both knew and told him about the books I had been reading. I was not trying to flatter anybody's fantasies. And I stopped myself from saying anything about my bank account, and I made no guarantees about "saving myself up" for someone if he would be kind enough to send me some fat cheques. Although the punters may have thought that I was subconsciously hiding my true feelings, it was not that way at all. I could have got myself married off loads of times – they were all good catches too – but I had made up my mind in advance and I stuck to my decision.

★

It was Michael Denhart's third visit to Pattaya. He was one of my nicest clients, really very generous and faithful. in that he could always be relied on for money. He was also one of my most persistent admirers, but in the most honourable sense.

It was our last meal together at the Mai Kai restaurant. He handed me an envelope, and I really did not know what to say when I opened it to find a Singapore International Airlines ticket to Frankfurt, made out in my name but bearing no date. I thought that he had really gone too far, especially as it was for one way only. My reaction must have seemed typically oriental.

"You're smiling inscrutably again," he said, with a touch of uncertainty in his voice.

Michael was good-looking, athletically built, but with an unusual softness in his features. He was comparatively pleasant to be with. Since he liked Far Eastern food it avoided one of the essential problems of spending time with a *farang*. And he played a lot of sport, which used up time during the day and meant that he was worn out at night. We got up early and spent the day riding, swimming, diving, sailing, water-skiing and parascending. We were very tired by the end of the evening, because we always had a good dinner and drank another couple of bottles of beer, and had early nights because we wanted to start off bright and early the next day. He mostly wanted sex first thing in the morning, when he felt refreshed after a good night's sleep and ready to get going for the day. We only really had time for a "quickie". That should have been all right with me, but I must admit I might even have enjoyed it a little if he had taken a bit more time over it. He did have a nice body, did not have a scratchy beard or bad breath, and above all was very careful about personal hygiene. He did not bother me during the night, and during the day he was entertaining to be with. Sex with him could have been good, clean fun for two.

Sometimes I wondered why he spent so much money on me and why I seemed to be the only one for him. Occasionally, I found him a bit slick and superficial. He would show me pictures of his life in Munich: in front of his BMW with the windsurfer on the roof; the salesman in his pinstriped suit

136

holding his attaché case; in his tracksuit with a sweat-band round his head; in front of his favourite bar in Schwabing. Young, dynamic, successful, sporty, attractive – a real ladies' man. But there would be moments in the evening when he would order another beer, slouch down and become inexplicably depressed. Then I would fulfil my part of the contract with real generosity, taking him by the hand, saying things to cheer him up and was quite surprised how concerned I felt for him. Perhaps his attachment to me had something to do with it. After all, about a year before, when he had come to Pattaya for the first time, he had proposed to me. I had refused with a smile. He did not press his case, but there were always tell-tale signs.

I put the airline ticket away. Seeing it irritated me, and I did not want to spoil his last evening in Pattaya.

★

In comparison to the system in Germany, which relies on pimps, the working conditions for the girls in Pattaya probably seem like paradise. Of course some of the girls were involved with ponces and drug rings, but most of them were able to work independently without being forced to surrender any of their money. The most important guarantee of this freedom was the romantic expectations of the tourists, since if a girl was expected to spend all day, every day with her holiday "husband" for weeks on end, it was difficult for any other sort of control to be exercised on her. And much of the pleasure for the client on this sort of holiday was to imagine that it was a real love affair of some kind. Brothels and massage parlours cannot satisfy this particular kind of fantasy.

However, so much money changes hands in Pattaya that there is no way the crime syndicates would not try to get their hand in. Everyone knows that organised crime in Thailand extends to the highest ranks of politicians, soldiers and the police. This is particularly true of drug rackets, prostitution and illegal labour.

So the Syndicate already had its finger on the trigger in Pattya. All the girls knew that the owners of the massage parlours, bars and discotheques were not honest business people. There was talk of protection rackets which also involved the smaller businessmen like taxi drivers and snack vendors. The waiters in the bars and restaurants were working under the most tremendous pressure, and we too could feel the noose around our necks. How long would it be before the Syndicate started asking us to pay "taxes"? And how much money would be left for us?

The Fantasy Club had a new manager, and this threatened to put an end to the easy-going working relationship between the various employees. The girls were afraid that the obligatory drinks coupons were going to double in price to fifty baht an evening. The waiters were now expected to achieve a bigger turnover, and in order to do this they kept forcing the customers to drink all the time. And of course the girls had to make their punters drink more too, and then it was up to them to look after the men once they were drunk.

"Everything's got out of proportion," complained Pim. "We're all on edge now. You used to be able to have a little chat with the waiters. Now they give you dirty looks if you don't try and get your pissed punter to have another beer. And that Chumpon, the new manager, he's a real swine, a vicious bastard. Just you ask the girls and see how many of them he's got his teeth into. One little sign, then he shuts the office door behind you, and half an hour later you come out looking like death. And the way he drinks! He can take the booze endlessly. I know he's got his eye on me, but I've made it quite clear to him that I know how to defend myself. And since you don't work here any more he needs me to do the dancing. If things get worse I might have to think about marrying my shy little Dane. Because, you know, sometimes I've really had enough of it all. What a pain it is to wake up in the morning trying to remember who you've got in bed next to you. I'd just like to climb up to the top of a palm tree and feel the cool wind in my face, blowing everything away and clearing my head."

One evening I had nothing to do, and decided to go and find some company at the Fantasy Club, in spite of all the things I had heard about the way things were going there. I had not seen some of the girls for a long time and I wanted to know how they were getting on. So that I would have lots of time to talk I went along at half past seven, and was the first girl to arrive. I bought my coupon and sat down on the empty terrace at one of Vichai's tables. He was one of the nicest waiters, and I ordered a large bottle of Singha beer to make him happy. But he seemed very tense. I soon found out why.

Chumpon, the new manager came out onto the terrace. He was placing his feet very deliberately one in front of the other. In his left hand was a glass of whisky with chinking ice cubes. He was a big man, but not exactly muscular, which was no doubt why he was silently shadowed by another man, obviously his minder. The two of them stood there, sur-rounded by a semi-circle of waiters. It was the day for doing accounts. Chumpon called each waiter up to him in turn and looked at the debits and credits on their lists, glass in hand. Only the first waiter had achieved his turnover target, and that only just. Chumpon tugged at his bow tie and poked him in the chest, telling him to him to do better next time. And from then on it got worse. Each subsequent waiter had turned over less than the one before. Each one tried to justify his failure. It was a cruel ritual and no excuses were accepted. The fourth waiter got hit in the throat for his trouble and was sent reeling. Chumpon, of course, had not even bothered to take the glass from his hand when he struck the blow.

I sat half hidden in the shade and watched with horror as this heartless bully punished these men who were all only doing their best to feed their families. Vichai was the last in line. He was hit twice in the eye, so everyone could see that he had been humiliated. Then he was writhing under the impact of a blow to the solar plexus. Then Chumpon pulled off a really dirty trick and kicked Vichai in the balls. I screamed out in anger. The boss and his sidekick turned slowly to me like a couple of turtles. I could feel Chumpon's eyes boring into me through the shadows. He came slowly up to me. His thug did not follow. After all, I was only a woman.

"Aha, madam who saw fit to leave us. To what do we owe the honour of this unaccustomed visit? Could we possibly talk a little business together? We have been so sorry not to have had this finest bead of jade in our midst. Would you come into my office for a moment? I have a proposition to make."

Of course his sly courtesy set off warning bells in my head. But what could I do? The manager had a powerful organisation behind him, which was not beyond putting my life in danger. All I could do was pretend to be obedient and pliable as bamboo.

His office door shut behind us. I noticed that it was padded with leather inside. Was that to keep the noise of the disco out, or to stop any noises from being heard outside? My thoughts were violently interrupted by a blow on the head that sent me flying against the treacherous softness of the padded door.

"You little piece of shit from out of the gutter, what do you think of that, you little cow, you cunt? I don't like to be disturbed when I'm doing business. Don't you like the way things are going? Are you trying to turn against me or something? Do you want to take on the Syndicate, then? Just ask, and we'll tear your cunt to pieces, you scum. We'll be keeping an eye on you from now on. Working for us, not on your own anymore. In the massage parlour. Got it?"

I was stunned. My brain could not take it. To be under someone else's control. Then I saw him look at me with a coarse gleam in his eye. His contempt was turning to lust. I was repulsed by his depravity, by this combination of hate and desire. He pushed me face down onto his desk, forcing my torso flat against the top with my groin caught against the corner. He pulled my skirt up, and tore my panties down to my knees. Then I pulled myself together, the terrified paralysis released its grip. Anger welled up in me.

"Come on then, you arse-fucker. Get it over with!"

I suddenly felt an excruciating pain in my anus. I twisted myself round and saw that what he was really doing was trying to ram a stubby stick of bamboo into me. He roared at me, showering me with spit.

"Turn back over!"

I jumped to the other end of the desk. Suddenly my mind was cool, icy, crystal clear. My brain was pumping thoughts at such a rate that I was conscious of a dual reality. Now in Pattaya, and the past in Khon Kaen. He came up to me, ready to pounce. I stayed right there and reached inside my handbag.

Khon Kaen – Pattaya. The same man. Pouncing on me in the same way. But then there is a twist in the story. The man suddenly stops. There is an uncomprehending look in his bloodshot eyes. He grips at his stomach. I pull out the blade of the flick knife from between his fingers. It leaves a trail of blood. He collapses on the floor and rolls over. I don't want to hear his moaning and groaning. I hide the knife in my bag and make for the door. I manage to get outside without anyone seeing me. I run through the brightly lit main street and reach the dark *soi* where our bungalow is. I'm in a hurry. I get together my passport, my bank book, some cash, the plane ticket and my toothbrush. I don't leave a message for Pim. The less she knows the better, if the Syndicate goes for her.

I run to the main street. Every second counts. An empty taxi comes along. I run up to the driver.

"How much to get to Bangkok? As fast as you can."

He can tell I'm in trouble. "Seven hundred?"

I jump into the car. The wheels spin as we drive off.

Is he going to die? It'll make no difference to me. They'll catch up with me wherever I go in the country.

Am I terrified at what I've done? No, not in the least. Along with my affection for the human race I have a hatred of anything that disturbs the balance of life. This hatred is dark and violent, but it is only the other side of my love. I even feel a sense of liberation. I have overcome all the obstacles that could have stopped me from doing what was right, all the anxieties and restrictions imposed by religion, the law, and a woman's place in society. That self-satisfied morality tolerates all the terrible things I have seen and experienced. It's not going to intimidate me now.

The driver has his foot hard down on the accelerator and is crouched over the steering wheel. Chonburi is now far behind us. We'll be in Bangkok around midnight.

Nearly all the time the driver has his eyes fixed on the road. The wet patches under his arms are spreading over his shirt. I can smell his acrid sweat. He's driving well, but I don't like the way he is taking sidelong glances at me every now and then. What is he thinking about me? And why is he looking at my body?

He finally blurts something out.

"You're very pretty. I'd only charge you five hundred if we could stop for a little while."

I am disgusted and turn to look out of the window, trying to make out the dark shapes that are flashing past.

"Come on, there's something up isn't there? Let's not make a fuss about it, sweetheart."

He puts a sweaty hand on my knee. I slowly open my bag, take out the knife and wipe off what's left of the blood with a paper tissue. The blade glitters in the light of the oncoming traffic. I hold the open knife in my hand. Beads of sweat appear on his forehead. Now he'll keep his mind on getting to Bangkok . . .

I asked the driver to stop in the Phrakanong district of the city, threw seven hundred baht at him, and waited till he had turned round and driven off up Sukhumvit Street. Then I hailed another taxi to take me to the Chinese quarter. Several times I looked behind me to check that I was not being followed by the driver from Pattaya, but he had well and truly gone.

Although it was late there was still lots going on in China-town. I felt safer there than anywhere else. I took a simple room in a small and clean family-run hotel, and then went to a little gaslit shop to buy myself an overnight bag and a change of underwear.

Even though I was exhausted I slept very badly that night. I was escaping from my homeland, crossing a precarious bamboo bridge into the unknown.

I was pleased when morning came, and I could get out of my twisted and sweaty bedclothes. There was a lot to be done, and I was going to have to keep my eyes open. By now the Syndicate would be closing in on me. I hoped I would still be able to slip through the net.

I took my bag and went to Silom Street to book a flight to Frankfurt at the SIA office. Luckily there were still places available. But wouldn't they be watching the airport? Most of the girls had neither passports nor enough money to fly out of the country. With any luck the Syndicate would think the same went for me and would be keeping an eye on the bus and train stations.

Then I went to the headquarters of my bank and closed my account. I transferred half my savings to my family, and for a moment I felt relieved, almost happy. I then had the rest transferred to an associate bank in Munich.

My next stop was the post office, where I sent a telegram to Michael Denhart. Now I had done everything I needed to do.

But what was the safest way of getting to the airport?

I went to the Erawan Hotel and sat reading for a while in the lounge. Eventually I strolled over to the reception desk and asked the girl in a casual voice whether she could book me a seat on the next limousine service for Don Muang. She did this straight away, and quarter of an hour later I was in an air-conditioned Mercedes on my way to the airport.

My heart was thumping so hard that I felt ill. I mixed in with a large group of Thai tourists happily wearing garlands of flowers. When we reached the check-in area I separated from the group and scurried off to the SIA desk. I was on the look-out for people watching me. My pulse began to race whenever I saw someone who looked suspicious. I had found out about the check-in system at the airline office and now tried to look as relaxed as possible, though I could not be sure whether I was succeeding.

At long last I was holding my boarding pass and making my way through passport control and customs. Was I safe now?

I had another hour of torture as we waited for the bus to take us to the plane. Only when I had fastened my seatbelt did I feel safe. No-one could drag me from this seat. And the husband and wife to my left would protect me. With all the tension I had nearly forgotten that I was flying for the first time. I could feel the aircraft accelerating on the runway, juddering as we got faster and faster. I would not have been surprised if we had carried on like that, skimming along over fields, deserts, mountains and sea. But then everything became distant and unreal. The roar of the jets pressed against my eardrums. The plane was whirring up to an even greater speed. Then I could not feel my legs any more and my stomach took off. At last I was surrounded by a timeless sense of peace as I snuggled up on the bed of clouds.

Naked in a cold land

The erotic oriental

Scraps of morning mist were still floating over the Rhine Valley, and slanting rays of sunlight were illuminating a landscape I had not expected to be so green. It was broken up by the concrete strips of motorway and the industrial plants which seemed to nestle harmoniously around the river. The plane was at an angle in the sky now, the brake flaps were down, and the air resistance could be strongly felt. "The Frankfurt Cross flyover," explained the friendly woman next to me. From above it was like a structural work of art, nestling in the green pine trees. Or was I seeing it all the wrong way round?

It was good to feel the wheels rolling along the concrete of the runway. I need to have the earth near to me. But I had to rid myself of the frightening impulse to flee from reality, the voice inside me saying, "It is time to till the field. What are you doing here?"

I had a fleeting impression of the passport control, the short verbal interrogation and the unfriendly customs men.

Michael was waiting for me in the crowd at the exit, a large bunch of long-stemmed roses in his arms. He was silent but happy. His eyes were watering. I laid my tired head on his shoulder for a moment.

The Frankfurt Cross is like a nightmare in a car. What happens if a driver's concentration wanders for a moment? The glittering perfection of the system is ruined, the perfect synchronisation destroyed. Why then do they flash their headlights, drive so close to the car in front and make threatening gestures? It stretches safety to the very limits.

I could only relax once we had passed Aschaffenburg, enjoying the ride through the valleys of the Spessart mountains, discovering idyllic little villages which were so old and dreamy. Around midday we crossed the high bridge over the Main at Würzburg. Michael was driving too fast, and a gust of wind pushed the car about a metre off course. It was as if we were suddenly being lifted off the bridge, and I did not know whether I wanted to fly upwards or plummet downwards.

Just before we got to Munich the traffic slowed. That was normal, so Michael told me. But soon we were in Schwabing. He lived in a nice area, in the Mandlstrasse near the Englische Garten park, right on the Eisbach. The flat seemed a little cold with its shiny lacquer and chrome, but a few souvenirs from Thailand livened it up.

He seemed to be so proud of me that he wanted to introduce me to his friends that very evening. Did his pride stem from his love for me, or did he just want to show off his exotic new creature? I did not care at the time because as yet I had no conception of the sort of life I was going to lead in this foreign world. But he seemed to be sure that I was going to stay with him.

The place where Michael and his friends met up almost every day was at a bar called Die Seerose (The Waterlily). That particular evening there were nine men and six women. The men were very happy that I could help make up the numbers. At first I was confused by the relationships between couples in the group, and I was to find out that the situation was indeed very complicated. When two members of the group had married, they had brought their new partners in with them. Then the bachelors left in the party were taken under the wing of the various women in the group.

It was real case of "change partners and dance", and people even got back together with their ex-lovers at times. It was all part of the *laisser faire* attitude in Schwabing, of the trendy liberalism there. But Michael told me with real sincerity that since he had met me all the "swinging" was over for him.

My entry to the group was celebrated with bottle after bottle of champagne bought by Michael. As the atmosphere became merrier and merrier, Michael suddenly told us that he was going to get the marriage announced at the registry office in the Mandlstrasse the very next day. I could not believe my ears. And then it was time for lots of sloppy congratulatory kissing. I noticed that the women were not exactly going wild with enthusiasm. I went off to the lavatory, washed my face and rinsed out my mouth in an attempt to get rid of the feeling of nausea. As I looked in the mirror I forced my mouth into a grin. Was this the answer to all my problems? I knew that it was better to be a free whore than the captive wife of a man I only regarded as a pleasant person to be with.

Why had he sprung such a surprise on me? I was angry and wanted to get my revenge on him for not taking account of my feelings. OK. I would marry him. I needed a permanent residence permit and enough time to sort out my future.

The marriage took place early one morning. One of the witnesses was Peter, who taught tennis in the Hirschau, where members of the group would meet up casually for a game on Sunday mornings. The other witness was Klaus Schrey, who was fat, quite a drinker, and earned a lot of money. He sold manufactured "precious" stones in pricey genuine settings, mainly to the wives of doctors, dentists and lawyers. Only an expert could tell the stones from the real thing. But Schrey did not lie to his customers, he sold the stones as expensive *artificial* products. He made the most money of any of Michael's friends because he was selling a product that was completely in keeping with the showy consumerism of the world I now found myself in. Thrifty whore that I was, I disapproved of it like some narrow-minded bank clerk.

The Seerose gang had widely varying incomes. Peter, as a tennis teacher, earned a pittance in comparison to Schrey. The others were a P.E. teacher at a high school, a draughtsman, an insurance salesman, the owner of a hairdressing salon and a shop selling jeans, and a computer programmer. Michael was an external consultant for an investment broker's. The financial position of the women was of particular interest to me. Not one of them was self-employed; they were a beautician, a salesgirl in a clothes shop, a secretary, a hairdresser and a clerk.

After a while I could assess the different earning potential of the various people in the group, as well as the outgoings of their lifestyle: a flat in Schwabing, fashionable new clothes each season, regular drinking sessions in the Seerose, and cars. The members of the group *had* to have a red BMW. Not necessarily the same model – Schrey had one of the big luxurious ones, of course – but a BMW it had to be. And then there were the leisure-time expenses. Conversation around the table at the Seerose was concentrated almost exclusively on leisure. Work was occasionally mentioned, but only as the way you spent the rest of your time. It was not done to talk about politics, though crude judgments were passed on the Reds, the Greens and Women's Libbers. However there was never any disagreement on these matters and everyone nodded their heads in a display of solidarity. If they spoke about Spain, it was not about the end of dictatorship, but about all the poofs in Torremolinos. And as far as Tahiti was concerned, why talk about child mortality when there are blue lagoons and palm-fringed beaches? They did not speak openly in front of me about Thailand and the Philippines, but I understood enough to learn that Philippino women were more in demand now because they spoke better English and were more western-ised. The group's view of the world divided it up into holiday areas, whose desirability was measured according to how expensive and fashionable they were. They were certain things that you had to do: go to Tuscany at Easter, spend a week glacier-skiing in the Stubai in June, have New Year in Southeast Asia. Majorca, which for ages had been mocked as the sort of place the cleaning woman goes for her holiday, was being rediscovered for its unspoilt west coast, and the Cinque Terre had gone down in everyone's estimation since one of the Seerose regulars had made the mistake of going there during the Italian holiday at *Ferragosto*.

I had grown up with the natural discipline of the land. Work was an important part of my existence, just like the joyful and pleasurable festivals at the temple. I only came across a contempt for work in foreigners, the tourists in Pattaya and Michael's friends. For all their frenzied leisure activity and endless rounds of sport I found the life of the Seerose gang to be dull and empty.

I was so eager to learn and needed to ask so many questions, but conversation with Michael and his friends always ended up going round in meaningless circles. I found it particularly hard to discuss anything with the women. All their conversation consisted of was clothes, make-up, holidays, their love-lives and other gossip. At least there were a few questions I could ask, about the clothes especially. I found that the women from the Seerose, like a lot of other German women, were incredibly provocative in their dress. As a woman and a prostitute I had a very simple attitude to sexy clothes: they were either for professional purposes or for tempting my lover in private. So the attitude of German women confused me. I remember one conversation where Eva, the hairdresser, was

149

making her feelings felt. She was angry about being propositioned by a Turk. I knew about the strict moral code of the
Muslims in south Thailand, and was not at all surprised to hear
this, since I thought that Eva dressed up like a real slut. She had
a carefully coiffured punk hairstyle and her dark eye make-up
had all the promise of a thousand and one nights. She put thick
purple lipstick on to transform her thin lips into pouting ones,
and she always had one blouse button too many undone, so as
to provide a more subtle come-on. In my opinion the very
short skirts she wore showed just a little too much of her
sturdy legs in their gold-trimmed cowboy boots. As she
complained about the "wogs" she really seemed to think she
was some stern and wrathful moral evangelist. I mischievously watched the grin on Schrey's lips as she let rip.

Schrey never made any pretences. He knew the rules of the
game, because he was the one who made them here. His
morality was based purely on his basic desires and the power
allowed him by his money. It had not taken him long to make
his intentions clear to me. When we were alone for a moment
he had told me straight out that he wanted me. I smiled,
saying:

"You know my line of business, but at the moment I'm not
available."

He just nodded and from then on treated me with a respect
he did not grant the other women. I assumed that he gave
money to other members of the group so that they could keep
up their style of living. There was no doubt that the women
could not have done it just on what they earned. But this
arrangement meant that he was at liberty to have the women
in the group as the mood took him. He did not make a great
point of it, but when he left the group and one of the women
got up to follow him, it meant that Schrey had made his choice
that time around. It made no difference to him whether one of
the women was "spoken for", and the other man in question
never made a fuss about having his woman commandeered.

This must have been because most of the men in the group had some sort of obligation to Schrey, whether through a loan or credit. Schrey kept quiet about his key role as financier for the group, but he obviously enjoyed his status as proprietor.

So Schrey had been one of our witnesses. That was all right with me since I found him almost likeable as the only honest person in this superficial world of frenetic enjoyment.

After the wedding we all went by bus to Wolfratshausen, where we were going to take a raft down the Isar as far as Thalkirchen. To help us celebrate Michael had hired a jazz band and a chef to do grills. A big barrel of beer was put on a stand in the middle of the deck.

It was a sunny, late summer's day, I was fascinated to sense autumn in the air for the first time in my life. Stretches of the route went through canals and special chutes built for rafts, and there were exciting moments, especially when rocks, like the Georgenstein, jutted into the river, and the steersmen at the front and back of the vessel had to work hard to avoid collisions. I sat behind the man at the bow, and as we came round every bend in the deep river valley I was delighted by a new vista. I recalled a trip I had once taken with B, when we were sprayed with water as we sailed in our sampan through the mountainous province of Chiang Rai. The images of the landscape and my memories had me under their spell, and I was far away from the goings-on around me and the occasion they were celebrating. Several times Michael tried to draw me into all the fun.

Every now and then someone would call out the Bavarian watchword "*Gaudi!*", at which everyone was supposed to go wild. You could not fend off the obligatory kiss without being called a spoilsport. I did not like the way this word told you what a bloody good time you ought to be having. I found it vulgar, childish and hypocritical – and I had yet to experience *Fasching* and Carnival. I thought of the Thai phrase *sanuk sabai,* which was so much more refined and intimate as an expression of shared goodwill and enjoyment.

Eventually I was forced to join in. You could hardly hear the music for the noise everyone was making as they drank and danced. Michael's friends were bringing their beer mugs together to wish each other's good health and kept on wanting to kiss the bride. I felt I was no longer my own mistress. Worst of all was the way Michael kept on giving me loving looks to tell me to look after the other guests. What had I let myself in for? I had fought so hard for freedom. Was I to lose it now through the pressure of other people's expectations? Was I just going to have to play the game? I felt as if I were allergic to being a good little housewife.

Things were beginning to go over the top – literally, in fact. Some of the guests had jumped into the river to show just how daringly drunk they were.

Schrey had taken off his shirt, and his rolls of fat made him look like the Michelin Man. He was running like an intoxicated satyr after the women, who were playfully fending off his advances.

Monika, the beautician, did not have much resistance to alcohol and she got tetchy after a certain stage. She was way past that stage by now. Her careful make-up was running with sweat, and she was obviously looking for a fight. When she saw that I was watching her she decided to home in on me. She was wearing high heels, which almost prevented her from moving at all on the boat, but that did not stop her from trying to totter towards me over tree-trunks which made up the raft. I was laughing inside as I watched her twisting about trying to keep her balance, and heard her swearing with pain when her foot slipped and she knocked her ankle against the stump of a branch. She was bursting with aggression by the time she got to me.

"Well then, the blushing bride! And was your pure white veil all in one piece? Or was it full of holes?"

It was quite obvious what she was getting at. The behaviour of the women at the Seerose had warned me. They had not liked me from the start.

"So this little slant-eyed thing just comes over here and gets her claws into the best man around."

I smiled inscrutably (as Michael would have it). This smile is disconcerting, even threatening for Europeans because they cannot understand it, but it is just a technique in our social behaviour, intended to create a buffer zone between individuals.

Monika pinched me on my arm and on the hip. "Well, it's all nice and firm. But you'd expect that from the natives. After all, they've only just come down from the trees." I laughed along with her, trying to get her a little more friendly. She moved up closer to me. "You know, I've heard that you oriental women know a thing or two about keeping your man. Charms, or something." I gave her a conspiratorial look and did my best to look serious.

"You take some sour milk, and add a dash of rose-water for taste and colour. Then you mix in a pinch of opium and a teaspoon of water buffalo's sperm. Then you beat in an egg with a hen's foot. Finally you whip up the drink for your beloved with a little menstrual blood, which he won't notice because of the rose-water."

Her head was so fuddled by alcohol that it took her a long time to catch on. Then she got really nasty:

"You shitface, you kinky little scrubber, you foreign tart!"

Suddenly there was the sound of someone roaring with laughter. I turned round to see Schrey leaning back and holding his stomach with glee. Had he heard the whole conversation or just the last part? Then poor, dear Michael came up, and called with a smile:

"You seem to be having a wonderful time!"

★

153

I still had no idea how my future was going to develop, but I was now at least doing something constructive again, because I had found life as a decorative little wife intolerable. I was now taking an advanced German course and took books out of the municipal library in the Hohenzollernstrasse if I could not buy them from Lehmkuhl's in the Leopoldstrasse.

It was a sunny autumn, and I took long walks in the Englische Garten, the Hirschau, and north and south along the Isar. The autumn colours were something new and fascinating for me, and I loved to drag my feet through the layer of leaves on the ground, which grew thicker and thicker as the season wore on. But I was also filled with sadness when I heard the crows in the now, almost bare trees heralding the winter with their chilling, mocking cries. At the same time I was also excited by the prospect of seeing snow for the first time. In Bangkok B had once sung me to sleep with a nursery rhyme about snowflakes.

Something happened to Michael's state of mind in the late autumn. He seemed to sink into a deep depression at times, started drinking too much, and so slept badly, having to get up several times in the night to quench the thirst left by the alcohol. Whereas before we used to go for an hour's tennis in the Hirschau no matter what the weather, I now had to fix up a game with one of his friends from the Seerose. His body began to lose its muscle-tone, he started to get paunchy, and his face looked puffy. I tried to find out what was wrong, but he just said "Forget it. Things will sort themselves out soon. All that matters is that you love me."

I sensed danger, realising that I was going to be asked to shoulder a responsibility I did not want.

Then things happened with relentless rapidity. Michael stopped going out to work. The bank was not allowing us any more credit, as I discovered to my embarrassment when I went to draw the housekeeping from Michael's account one day. Then notice to quit immediately came from the estate managers and several official demands for payment arrived. I asked Michael to tell me what was going on, and he revealed that the managing director of the investment brokers he worked for had staged a false bankruptcy. And Michael had been implicated too.

No more money coming in. No credit, no savings. This was how things really were behind the glossy facade.

"What are we going to do now, Michael?"

"I've asked Schrey round this evening. He's the only one who can help me. Make yourself pretty and cook something nice."

Schrey soon caught on that a favour was going to be asked of him. I could feel him sniffing out the situation. He was friendly enough, but more reserved than usual. I had gone to a lot of trouble to make a good dinner, cooking his favourite sweet and sour pork. He complimented me politely on the meal. Then he got down to business. "So then, Michael, tell me what you're up to. I know what's happened to your firm. You could smell something rotten in those Canadian investments from a mile off. So now you're in the shit."

Michael nodded his head pathetically, hunched up over his wineglass. His voice came out brokenly:

"I need sixty thousand marks. And straight away. Otherwise it's prison."

Schrey stared at him. He did not look unfriendly, but there was no hint of compromise in his face. Michael could not even look him in the eye. I really felt sorry for him.

"You know of course that you still owe me thirty thousand. And since you're not creditworthy anymore, I'll be wanting my money straight away. But you also know how I like to help my friends from the Seerose. But you're really naughty little creeps, the way you play at being big boys and then expect Daddy to help you out. Now, as far as the girls are concerned it's all part of my obligations as a gentleman, but surely you of all people should be able to get by on your own."

I felt so sorry for Michael that I looked pleadingly at Schrey. Didn't he feel anything at seeing Michael sobbing with his head in his hands?

"Well, I have a suggestion for you. Just one." He looked at the tips of his fingers. "I'll give you the thirty thousand. If you don't take up my offer, the amount owing is due as of tomorrow. If you do, then I relinquish all claims in writing. But I want one thing of you." Saying this he raised his eyes slowly to me. "I want your wife to spend tonight with me."

Michael froze. He looked disbelievingly at Schrey.

"But . . ."

Schrey was abrupt. "That is my last offer, as I told you already."

Michael collapsed in a whimpering heap. An ominous silence fell upon the room.

Michael was incapable of making a decision, so it was up to me now. A night with Schrey? A routine job. But how would Michael cope with the destruction of his romantic dreams?

And if I did not go with Schrey, what then? Michael would be finished straight away. He would be reduced to a social nonentity. He had put money into me. I may not have become his loving wife, but I thought it only fair to stand by him now.

I stood up, and stroked Michael's head. Schrey also got up. Michael had broken into harsh, dry sobs. I thought of the parched drought wind blowing through the bamboo and making the withered leaves rustle in the rain-starved Isan.

Schrey seemed to be glowing with excitement and full of confident anticipation as we drove in his car to the Osterwald-strasse.

"I've been waiting for this for a long time. From the moment I saw you. I knew I could only have you by paying for it, but that never bothered me. As far as I'm concerned it doesn't matter whether a woman's being paid or doing it of her own free will."

He had a round water-bed in the middle of the room. It stood on a white carpet that was so thick you sank up to your ankles in it, and had strong spotlights shining down onto it. The water inside the clear plastic split the light up into countless rays and the whole thing glittered like a crystal chandelier. The rest of the room was in darkness and the only other furniture was a leather armchair and a stack hi-fi system. Schrey put on a tape and disappeared into the bathroom. "Beethoven's Fifth!" he called out. The music reverberated around the bare surface of the room. The reproduction was so perfect that it seemed as if all the musicians were somehow there, like invisible ghosts.

Schrey came back out, wearing nothing but a dressing gown with Chinese embroidery. He threw a bundle of clothing at me. "I bought those at a naughty little shop in the Hohenzollernstrasse. They've been rather special for me, because I've always hoped you'd wear them for me one day. All the gear's yours to keep, of course."

He had given me the works: fishnet stockings, bodysuits, leotards, patent leather hot pants, and so on. There was even a snakeskin jumpsuit, lace wristbands and other bits and pieces. So I was back in business. And what a price – thirty thousand marks a night!

I began to undress as Schrey pushed his chair back from the glow of the water bed. He sat there with a lecherous grin on his face like a fat and good-tempered Chinese Buddha suffering from high blood pressure. His gown had been left half-open, showing off the triangle of fat flesh between his thighs and stomach with his little penis sticking up in the middle.

He asked me to try on various articles of clothing. To begin with he told me how I ought to move, then he just sat back and watched like some happy chubby-cheeked schoolboy. He was a self-centred, systematic man. It was going to be a hard night.

The water bed bubbled and wobbled beneath me as I did my erotic gymnastics. I was going to ache the next day. Schrey was lost in concentration like a tantric yogi. He did not touch me, which I found surprising, but just sat there taking it all in. His intention seemed to be to spend the whole night with his erection on the point of orgasm – the greatest feat in the Karma Sutra. He probably wanted to get the best value for his thirty thousand marks.

As the dawn broke the light over the bed began to soften a little. That night I had made an erotic interpretation of all the nine Beethoven symphonies. Thanks to my professionalism I had been able to put thoughts of Michael out of my head, but now I was filled with disquiet.

Schrey's eyes had become glazed. He finally got up and lay down on the bed. My right hand was shaking as I reached for his organ, which was now purple with turgidity. Even before I touched it he ejaculated.

I stood up, since I was in a hurry to go, although I was too well-trained not to hand Schrey some paper tissues.

I slipped into my clothes, put all the bits and pieces he had given me in a plastic bag and bowed to him as I went. "I'm worried about Michael." But he was past caring, having fallen into an exhausted sleep.

There was not a taxi to be had. I got more and more worried. I tried not to think of all the terrible things that could happen, but my legs began to move faster and faster.

Autumn rain began to fall from the leaden sky in the murky half light between night and day. I tore up the stairs to find a piece of paper stuck to the front door of the flat. "Please call Police Station 5." Beneath the message was the phone number. The blood was rushing to my head, my ears were throbbing. I tried to get through for five minutes, but got the engaged tone every time. Then I was connected.

"I am very sorry, but I have some bad news for you."
Michael had driven at top speed through the railings of the bridge over the Isar on the Föhring ringroad.

★

I asked myself endlessly whether I could have prevented Michael's death. Perhaps, but only if he had really been able to feel that I loved him. He just had not been able to convince himself enough.

The Institute of Forensic Medicine found there to be a high alcohol content in his blood. I had to admit cynically to myself that it was lucky for me. His life assurance company had done some research and had suggested that it may have been suicide, but the alcohol count finally decided the matter and they had to pay up. Schrey did not say a word about what had happened that night when they asked him. Only later did I realise that I had narrowly escaped having to find the money to pay Michael's debts.

It was strange that Michael had only recently increased the sum of his life assurance by a substantial amount. So I was still left with a lot of money once I had sorted out his affairs.

Well then, you tough little whore, I said angrily to myself, your men suffer, they even die, and you just watch your bank account grow.

I left Munich.

I had already been on a trip to Hamburg, and from what I had seen there I thought it would be a better place to live.

You can choose between three hundred Far Eastern restaurants there, and a lot of orientals live in the Hanseatic town. You can feel that it has a tradition of welcoming the world.

And there is St. Pauli with its prostitutes, somewhere seamen all over the world dream about. I could belong there.

And the River Elbe, the umbilical cord to the sea, and countries over the sea, and my home.

She-Tiger

Sex, Power and Pity

The muffled hooting of the foghorns came through the morning mist. Looking from my window I saw the Fischmarkt, the River Elbe and the harbour, their hazy outlines seeming to belong to another world.

Little tugs like pilot fish were guiding big tankers and container ships along the channel. Where were the ships going?

My thoughts followed the ships through the fog and out into the sunlight where they could dry their wings and fly more lightly and much faster the thousands of nautical miles to the tropics, landing on white sand which is softer than the water could ever be. There mangroves, lianas, orchids, rain-trees, alders, flame trees, hibiscus and bougainvillea grow in abundance. I opened the window, as if ready to take my flight. But the dampness of the fog pushed me back to the warmth of my flat.

I had rented a four-room flat on the Pinnasberg with a view of the Elbe. Behind it was St. Pauli, and the Reeperbahn was only a few minutes away. I had made it comfortable and homely with rattan and bamboo furniture, big yucca palms, delicate bamboo shrubs, asparagus plants and lots of other

161

greenery. When the dirty winter weather got too oppressive I would put on some music, take a book and snuggle myself up in a corner of my warm little "bamboo grove".

I got to know all the sides of Hamburg, a city of contrasts. After days of miserable rain there would be fresh breezes from the sea, dispersing the clouds and clearing your lungs. I learned too to distinguish between the Hamburgers, the people of the city, and the Hanseatics. I liked the noisy Hamburgers, who though sometimes a bit rough on the outside, were warm inside: the women shopkeepers, the workers from the shipyards and the stallholders from the Fischmarkt. But the Hanseatics, with their airs and their Elbchausee snobbery, were not to my taste at all.

I had already spent three days at the city museum, finding out about the city's network of waterways, made up of the arms of the rivers Elbe and Alster and the canals. I had also taken three trips round the harbour, and was amazed by how exciting engineering could be. When the mechanism of a dry dock was explained I really got quite worked up about it, the idea behind it seemed so simple, yet so effective.

I began to love the Elbe. I called it *Menam*, Mother of the Waters, although the river was really more of a foul old wicked stepmother who poisoned any living thing she encountered. Once I went as far as Wedel and wandered back to the Fischmarkt from there. The rain did nothing to spoil the pleasure I got from exploring. As I came past the Blankenese Süllberg I imagined all the old sea captains with their white beards who had come here to retire after withstanding many a typhoon on the misnamed Pacific Ocean, but now looked longingly at the departing ships, wondering where they were heading for with their horns sounding, calling for the wind's embrace.

I drank a glass of grog with Tommie at Dill sin Döns on the banks of the river. Tommie was snoring to himself, perhaps dreaming about what fun he would have making eyes at the ladies in their mink coats when they came down from the Elbchausee at the weekend. I sat watching the ships on the river, which were passing alarmingly close by.

And what about the men on board? Was each sailor leaving a weeping girl in every port? Was he looking forward to seeing another one in Rio, Hong Kong, Manila, Singapore or Bangkok? Was he happily remembering the big fat mamma in the Herbertstrasse who had taken that nice young man who paid so well between her thick legs, and so fulfilled one of his most cherished dreams? Or was he hung over, left with a nasty taste in the mouth because the nervous tart the night before had smelt just as nasty as the bar at the docks where he had picked her up?

I came to Teufelsbrück and took a detour via the Jenisch Park and Övelgönne, and dreamed of living in one of the little toy houses which looked so inviting as the lights began to come on in their cosy front rooms.

In the evening the Fischmarkt is lonely and unfriendly and only the left-over smell tells you that it is so busy in the morning. I went into the Haifischbar to warm myself up a little and had a suspicious welcome from the girls in there, who eyed me up and down coldly. I felt sorry for them, having to walk the streets with so little on. I wondered how many of them had blocked-up Fallopian tubes from the chills they must have caught. They used to stand there in the rain, like bewitched signposts pointing the way to the citadel of the Great Pimp Nosferatu, bathed in the shimmering triangle of light beneath the street lamps, then to be shrouded in a veil of mist. When the lights of a car approached, the veil would be lifted with impatient and obscene gestures of enticement. They would stand on one leg and raise the other one, moving it outwards, lifting their short skirt to reveal the curly hair beneath, dewy with drops of condensation.

In a street parallel to the Reeperbahn is the Bangkok, a Thai restaurant. There I met Chintana, another woman from the Isan. She became a very useful source of information about the tough, organised world of the red-light district in Hamburg, and so could help me to slip through all the traps laid by the procurers.

Chintana's eyes were surrounded by crow's-feet. They looked dead and world-weary. She had worked in Patpong Street in Bangkok where she had met a German she followed to Hamburg. They got married, but everything went wrong and they ended up on bad terms. She left him, and was faced with no other choice but to go back on the game.

Chintana had experienced many sides of the Hamburg scene. She had worked in bars, sex clubs, saunas and brothels. Now she was a dancer in a peepshow. She disliked work in the bars and clubs the most.

"You're paid a basic, one hundred marks a day, and the rest you get as a percentage of the drinks. And if your customer buys a bottle of champagne, then the price includes a session in a private room, and you have to go on your back on the carpet in there. That's taken as said, but it wouldn't be so bad if it wasn't for the mood they create. The punters come to the bar instead of the knocking shop because they like to pretend there's a bit of romance. They want to kid themselves that they've really pulled you. So you've got to put up all the time with their groping and canoodling. Yek! I can't do it without booze and Valium any more."

Then Chintana had gone to work in a brothel. There she earned more and felt less under stress, since it did not seem so private and intimate. It may seem surprising, but in fact most prostitutes find work in a brothel "cleaner" and more professional than in a bar or club, where some sort of intimacy is supposed to be struck up beforehand. In a brothel sex is on a production line. It is soullessly commercial and a matter of getting through the customers as quickly as possible. The girls may start off by blowing seductive kisses, making eyes at the clients and saying "How about it, sweetie?" but that is as far as the romance goes. Then it's down to business: "Normal", with or without a condom, licking, breast touching, S & M – every part of the body and every method has a fixed price, and it all has to be done as quickly as possible. Prostitutes are small businesswomen with a skilled service to offer and their mentality is in keeping with this. They are thrifty to the point of miserliness, obsessed with money, and they have a small-minded set of "morals". I was always amazed by the other girls' contempt of their customers. I suppose it is true that after working in mass-market prostitution for a while all you see are caricatures of men, who stare at you lecherously; you get alcoholic fumes breathed all over you, and you have to put up with the cheesy and acrid smell of urine-stained under-pants. All you hear from these men are stupid comments, dirty jokes and incoherent grunts. And the sum total of all these impressions is a disgust for the punters. During my time in Germany I have met many women who, though real tramps and social outcasts themselves, have behaved aggressively and dimissively towards cleanly and soberly dressed Turks. It was probably a suppressed sense of self-accusation and guilt which they turned against the men to make themselves feel better. In Hamburg I hardly met a single girl with whom I could openly discuss the real reason why we were there – prostitution. Of course, professional details and problems were discussed and the vice squad were criticised for their "arbitrary" raids, but I hardly ever heard one of my fellow prostitutes ask why ours is "the oldest profession in the world". Why were whores seen as saints at the same time? Why were they also priestesses? Why did the philosophical hetaerae sell their bodies? Can prostitution be explained only in terms of dire social necessity? Or can psychological concepts like erotomania, instability, weakness of will and masochism also be considered as factors? And why do men keep going to prostitutes? Why does the whore turn up again and again in the literature of the world? Can it be explained in terms of the more superficial desires and motivations in men, of physical and social defects, or of immaturity of character?

I was shocked to find out that my colleagues were more than just uninterested in all these questions – they actively dismissed them. Their automatic contempt of the clients is a result of their petit-bourgeois conventionality. Their pimp, more often than not a hard, exploitative and violent man, becomes the respectable husband of their fantasies. All that the pimp does is provide some sort of "protection" as far as the scene is concerned, and perhaps it flatters the woman's sense of pride and vanity if he is a good-looking guy. I visited some of the other girls at home and was surprised to discover that they generally had all the trappings of lower-middle-class Germany: the canary, the picture of a gypsy girl, the rutting stags over the settee, and the white lacquer-finish bedroom suite with pink sheepskin mats by the bed. And how many times must I have heard one of the girls say, "In a few years I'll get my old man out of the business. Then I can live like a normal person."

Chintana's hatred of the customers finally forced her to leave the Eros Centre on the Reeperbahn, since she could no longer bear to have a man near her. By the end even the Valium could not stop her from feeling sick at the prospect of touching one. What was left of her feelings was now directed at women. I could tell that from the way she looked me up and down.

After all I had heard about St. Pauli I was now at something of a loss. I might have actually enjoyed dancing at the Salammbo, but you needed references and contacts I just did not have at that time.

Chintana now worked in a peepshow. She went on three times an hour. One of these performances was a lesbian duet, which was always announced by cashier and disc-jockey in very provocative terms.

"If you do the lesbian bit with me, you'll get two hundred marks for the seven-hour shift. And if you want, you can have private appointments with punters in the solo booth."

Not without some hesitation I said that I would have a go. I felt that in itself the peepshow was a revolution in the history of prostitution. It fits in with the general policy of organised money-making. Instead of labour-intensive service for an individual client you had one dancer on a revolving podium surrounded by eighteen booths with a slit to look through and a plastic bin in each. It all has to be cleaned regularly and is carefully supervised by the authorities. Easy-care satisfaction. The woman's body remains untouched, so why people are trying to put a stop to peepshows "in the interests of women", I really do not know. After fast food we now have a fast fuck – all synthetic, of course. You eat a quick hamburger for lunch, and then you go off to get quick fulfilment of another basic human need. You eat, drink and have an orgasm all within your half-hour lunch break or in the time before you take your train home to the suburbs.

"Sorry, darling, I missed the train again. Has my dinner gone cold?"

The peepshow is the triumph of materialism. The slot for the money becomes a symbolic vagina. You sort out the girls by putting in one mark and then you wait till the sexiest one comes on. You have a five mark piece ready in your hand, because she is on for five minutes. There is an atmosphere of nervous excitement as the flap of the panel opens like a magic lantern. There is a quick changeover on the revolving plat-form, and the new girl spreads her cloth down on the carpet and undoes two press-studs at the crotch of her catsuit. Then she flashes her genitals invitingly at the spectators, whose faces come forward out of the darkness and press their noses against the glass. Their eyes pop out of their heads and their faces wobble as they work their hands back and forth down below. They often try to break out of their cell, and lick desperately at the cold glass.

And then there are the solo booths. The customer notes the number of the girl he wants to have for himself, goes into the "monkey cage", presses a button with the number on, and waits till the girl he has asked for comes into the little room with the vinyl-covered chair. He now has to put in five marks every two minutes so that the light stays on in the part of the room where the woman goes, which is divided off by a clear plastic wall. This has got holes or slits in it, so that the customer can say exactly what he wants her to do.

During the four weeks I had agreed to work at the peep-show I spent most of my time in the solo booths, which was a sign of my desirability. I often used to wonder which one of us was the monkey, him sitting there masturbating, grimacing and groaning in his section, or me, opening my vulva and displaying my anus, the two actions which were all most of the customers could think of to ask me to do.

I spent four tortuous weeks in the peepshow. I only stayed there because I was determined to play the game in my new professional milieu. But I would escape back to my flat or go on long walks by the river just as soon as I could. I decided to try a different tack.

Chintana came to visit me one evening. I made some tea and we sat in front of the french windows to the balcony and looked out onto the Elbe.

"I'm going down to the Ruhr and was wondering if you wanted to come too. My friend Ruang has written to me. There's a carnival committee there putting on a "Siamese Night". All we've got to do is dance, nothing else. And they pay good money. I've done that kind of thing before. Believe you me, if you really want to know what German men are all about, you should go to one of these carnival stag shows."

B had told me once about the customs of Fasching, their Shrove carnival. He had explained the almost mythical status of this festival, how it meant everybody could let off steam caused by psychological, sexual and social pressure. He had also said that the maternity wards were always especially busy nine months later. In the past the Catholic church must have been very successful at keeping everybody under control, perhaps because it understood human nature so well, ruling with a combination of lavish sensual indulgence and strict inquisitorial zeal. It had always supported these few days of madness, this pagan outbreak of grotesque frenzy when the confines of morality were forgotten. But then the Church had Ash Wednesday up its sleeve, time for repentance, falling on your knees for forgiveness and ashes on the head. I found this cruelly contradictory. Its uncomfortable twist had nothing to do with the complementary unity formed by the *yin* and *yang* of my oriental culture.

B had also told me that the meaning of the festival had long ago got lost in a dreamy parade of fancy dress, silly sexual hanky-panky and "We're all lads together" jollification.

But I was curious to see some of this stupidity, because it would mean a release from the organisation and systemisation of everything in Germany. At least I stood to find out something more about German men, so I went with Chintana to Bottrop.

The hall where the "Siamese Night" was to take place was still filled with the stale smells of the previous night's carnival celebrations. Still, tonight there would be fresh sweat and alcohol to cover over the old stench. At one end of the room was the stand for the Committee of Eleven. On either side of it stood a sad-looking plastic palm. So it was up to us to provide the tropical atmosphere. The organiser had asked Ruang, Chintana and me to put on tiger-skin leotards. As we walked onto the stage we were greeted with rhythmic clapping. Suddenly we were bombarded with aggressive cries of "Get 'em off!"

The band who were called "Die drei Besuffkopps" (The Three Boozers) began to sing. "In Bangkok the nights are long . . ." Then the president of the Committee of Eleven introduced the compère for the evening, "Our Jupp", who was wearing a bright blue and white striped shirt and a great big baby's dummy round his neck. In his right hand was a pink plastic potty, which was half filled with beer. Every now and then he took a mouthful of it while the spectators wished him a raucous "*Prosit!*" Then Jupp began to tell his jokes at full pelt.

"You must all have read the one in the papers about the o.a.p. in Bangkok who popped his clogs in the arms of a lady of pleasure. His last word was not "Brandy", but "Randy". Then the angels carried him off. And now you know why they call Bangkok the City of Angels!"

Was this what it was going to be like all evening? Then the "Drei Besuffkopps" launched into a poetic little ditty: "Mitsou, Mitsou, Mitsou, Mitsou, The girl with the sweetest cherry is you." Then Jupp took a suggestive gulp of "cherry wine". I suddenly remembered how a Japanese girl had been elected Carnival Queen in Düsseldorf that year. A storm of indignation had burst out, there was even talk of "an offence to German womanhood." The Queen of the Fools had to be a girl of pure German extraction, and certainly was not to be allowed to take part in stag nights such as this where it was all right for oriental sex objects to be on show live on stage.

Jupp was really in the swing of it now. "My neighbour's married to this Siamese woman who doesn't speak a word of German. But he's had seven sons by her. Which just goes to show you what a man can do when he hasn't got his wife nagging him all the time."

And then it was the "Drei Besuffkopps" again, whose music we were supposed to be dancing to. They were singing their big hit of the moment, which went, as far as I can remember: "Bang in Bangkok, tralala, next stop Pattaya . . ."

Ruang and Chintana did not seem to be too bothered by it all. Perhaps they did not understand everything. My stomach was turning. I would have liked to take a flame thrower and clear the hall of this vermin. Dirty little runts. Safety in numbers, I suppose.

"Now our three little beauties from the jungle must try and say something in German. What can you manage then? *Heil Hitlel. Hip! Hip! Hullah?*"

I was bursting with rage, but Jupp just kept on going. He came up close to the microphone, and slid his finger along between his lips to make a squelching noise.

"Know what that is?" he asked. "A Siamese woman sliding down the bannisters!"

I could not take any more and stormed out, leaving that ship of fools to sink in its own bilge.

★

I spent a long time working out my "terms of employment", which I was determined to stick to: Hours – 7 p.m. to 1 a.m.; a five day week, Tuesday evening to Sunday morning; no more than one client per night, even if he only takes up an hour of my time; basic charge – 1000 marks per six hours or any fraction of that time. This was a pretty tall order, but I did not think it was beyond me. I had money behind me, and I did not have a pimp forcing me to work at any price. So I could consciously aim to achieve the objective I had set myself as early on as Khon Kaen: "disembodied" prostitution by means of a simulated but enticing sexual performance.

171

Of course, what I needed now was a certain kind of client. Not a sailor or docker with rough hands and at the most two hundred marks in his pocket who was just out for a screw. What I wanted were successful and well-to-do men with status, even power, and "refined", perhaps special, tastes. I sensed that limitlessly ambitious men, the power-hungry workaholics, the "pillars of society" in politics, business and the arts often have a sexual demon whispering in their ear. Their often morbid energy is openly displayed, but they have to temper it for the sake of public approval. Behind it there is often a world where dark forces are at work, the negative image of the public spotlight. This is the domain where vengeful spirits punish dishonesty, where the Furies chase the hardened cynic, where thieving and leprous hands extort the toll for ruthlessness, where torturers whip up the agonies of uncontrolled longing for power, where the castration complex is deepened by the swinging of sickles, where the mother's womb draws in the child, only to expel him, where the full breast runs instantly dry.

★

"A penny for your thoughts.
Or just let me guess . . ."

These were the opening words of the advertisement I put in the "Contacts" column of the *Süddeutscher Zeitung, FAZ* and *ZEIT*. I also obtained a list of high-class addresses – lawyers, specialist doctors and senior consultants, top managers and so on. I sent one thousand discreetly worded letters on dusky pink deckle-edged paper with a picture of bamboo in purple. I also stuck on an alluring photograph of me. Of course, this got the vice squad onto me, but I behaved like a good girl, and we sorted things out.

My telephone started ringing at all hours of the day, so I bought an answering machine, asking the caller to leave his name and number. Over the next few weeks I had about three hundred preliminary telephone conversations, and from them about one hundred and twenty rendezvous, either on neutral ground or in my flat. With all the organising I had to do I often forgot what the whole thing was really about – sexual hang-ups.

The conversations, call them diagnosis sessions if you will, were surprisingly candid and to the point. It would seem that I showed so much interest, empathy and professional skill – not to mention a readiness to participate in their fantasies – that the prospective clients generally felt at ease straight away.

During these conversations I got rid of the men who got too much of a shock when I named my price, and also the ones whose desires were too, shall we say, *carnal*.

There were certain types that I knew I did not want:

The fellatio type, who has a castration complex of the most intense kind, and who enjoys the self-torture of subjecting himself to the very thing he fears most. Sura, a Thai call girl I knew in Hamburg was an expert on this. "You know, two thirds of them only want that, and without a rubber, of course. I mean, there are such things as banana-flavoured rubbers, at least that makes it bearable. But they want it all *au naturel*. They shove their cocks so hard into your mouth that it hurts your gums. But I've got a little trick. I slow down their jerking by pushing the other way with one hand and squeezing their balls with the other. If the fella's getting too carried away I crush his bollocks a bit, and say, "Sorry, I was getting too excited!" That way he learns to behave like a good boy. And you know why they won't wear a rubber? Because you're meant to swallow everything when they come. What I do is swill it about a bit, and when I've still got my mouth full I squeal, "More, more! It's the sweetest cream!"

The "normal fucker". A lot of the high–class call girls like this type best, surprisingly enough. Perhaps because he is not all that common among the clients of expensive prostitutes, and perhaps because he seems so "nice and normal" to a girl who is actually engaged in pretty varied and strenuous activity for much of the time. But I do not like this type precisely because he *is* "nice and normal". It can easily get far too personal with him. He falls straight in love with you, promises to take you away from it all, and gets horribly gallant. He has read *Suzie Wong* and feels he has to romanticise the world of prostitution he is so strongly drawn to. And since he wants to make it all into something conventional, he starts playing at being the gentleman and tells you what you ought to do with your life.

And of course, I do not like the macho types, the self-centred tightarses, the men with an anal fixation, the kind who likes it "the French way", in short, anybody who forces himself upon me, and who offends my nostrils and taste buds. And I do not like a frequently requested form of cunnilingus, where mustard is applied first and then licked off, although I must admit that it amuses me to think of it as the *hors d'oeuvre* to a cannibalistic main course.

What I wanted was to use my sex appeal, my youth and my gifts as an actress and dancer to create a wild show which would delight the customers and make me a lot of money. I did not want men who just wanted to get their hands on me, but ones who would see me as some sort of sexual icon, the image of their fantasies, or as an untouchable flame glowing in the dark night of their passions. And I carefully built myself up a clientèle of this kind, ending up with about twenty-five regulars, too many, in fact, to see them as often as they would have liked. But I needed to have a reserve in view of natural wastage, and I needed a wide range of customers so that I did not become financially dependent on a few, or even on just one. Many of the Thai call girls I knew had come to be like mistresses, and were afraid of being left without an income at one fell swoop. And lots of my clients begged me to become their mistress. The more often I smilingly refused, the more insistent they became, and the more money they offered me. I took their money and kept on refusing. I was calling all the shots, making restrained and sparing references to favours I would do them, so getting them even more hooked. This was my special little trick, not a cruel one in my opinion, since if you increase desire, the moments of fulfilment are all the more ecstatically intense.

The nature of their sexual needs, and the delicate relation of these needs to their position in society, meant that I was called upon to be very discreet. They could all tell that I would keep their secrets, and so most of them revealed their identities and details of their personal lives. In the final analysis I was their confidante, and knew more about their deepest darkest secrets than the women they were married to. But some of them retained their mystery.

One of these men was Mr X. That was what I called him since he never told me his real name. And I only ever spoke once to him, at the beginning of our arrangement, when he telephoned me and explained concisely, precisely, and without the faintest hint of embarrassment, exactly what he wanted me to do. From then on I met him every Tuesday evening at ten. If he was not coming he sent me a lined envelope with a one thousand mark note. If there were several thousand marks in the envelope, then I could calculate for how many weeks he was not going to be able to turn up.

I only ever met him in the dark, on the dot of ten, at the outer limits of the red-light district. It was at the steps in the Fischmarkt, near Schorch's, the strange bar where the sailors go. I had told the girls who worked there that I was not trespassing on their patch. Because of the dark, rain and fog it was difficult to see more than that he had a finely chiselled face and was greying at the temples. What was more, he always had the collar of his coat turned up, his Homburg was pulled down over his eyes and he stood out of the lamplight when he handed me the envelope with my money in it. In return I would open up the short black patent leather coat he had specified, and in the shimmering lamplight he would see that I was wearing the skimpy bra and rubber knickers too. Then I would walk about five paces away to stand at the lonely riverside. The heels of my patent leather boots clicked along the street, guiding him, so that as I then ran back and forth in front of him he could flash a dim pocket torch on me. He stood there quietly as I strutted about, swinging my hips, stroking my breasts and tilting my head flirtatiously to one side like some two–bit tart. But that was how he wanted it. I still don't know whether he brought himself off as he watched me or whether I just inflamed his imagination. All I know was that the light from the torch ran over my body, almost as if it were stroking it. And I am not afraid to be out in the dark, close to the rushing waters of the Elbe, because I always have an old friend with me – my flick knife from Pattaya.

The appointment with Mr X lasts almost exactly an hour. Then he switches his torch off and I hear his footsteps moving away. But one of my clients takes up even less of my time.

P.M. is the boss of his own engineering consultancy, and is an internationally renowed specialist in the construction of dams. His special kink is really rather sweet. His stimulation is brought about through aural and visual means. I dance for him, and he watches me as he also listens to the music which rhythmically builds his excitement and finally brings it to a climax – Ravel's *Bolero*.

I start off meditatively playing with my clothes, swaying dreamily to the subtle rhythm. Then, as the music begins to crescendo, becoming more and more insistent, I begin to run

She-Tiger

my hands impetuously over my body. He moans a little, moves his hand compulsively to his organ, and begins to rub it in time with the music. And when the music reaches its abrupt end, evaporating into silence, I fall exhausted to my knees, panting just a little, while my client sits there like Rodin's *Thinker* – though his hand is not under his chin, but doing its work between his legs.

And he is groaning gently to himself, as if something wonderfully and indescribably beautiful had just happened to him. I smile at him, delighted at my performance, but I also feel just a little happy for him too. We wink to each other as we say goodbye with a drawling Hamburg "Tschüss!" As he goes I call out the Bavarian greeting "Servus". He, as a proud citizen of Hamburg, thinks that the Balkans start once you get past the Harburg mountains, and he shakes an admonishing finger at me.

There are also more demanding customers. One of them is Professor K., senior consultant at a Catholic hospital in Westphalia. As a young man he worked at a missionary station in Indochina. I do not know whether he discovered his special preference out there, or whether he went there to indulge it. *Mai pen arai*, be that as it may, his feelings were now dominated by a contradiction between the holy missionary and the unholy lecher.

I played the little heathen with him, the innocent and exotic child of nature, who was to be "civilised" by his missionary zeal. The Professor visited me every two weeks, and I had to prepare myself particularly carefully for him, because if even the slightest detail was amiss he became bad tempered, and as a punishment he withheld the envelope with my money in it. If I was a good girl he added to the agreed sum.

The decor for the little scene was simple: a screen, two little stools and a small table, all made of bamboo. I then completed the set with a tall yucca palm. I wore a short navy blue pleated skirt and a white blouse, standard school uniform in Southeast

177

Asia. I went barefoot. I would skip into the "classroom", only to be scolded by my strict schoolmaster. I had to work very hard not to let a smile creep onto my face or even burst into laughter. It was really too funny, but a pleadingly serious, even sad, look in the professor's eyes stopped me from losing control. The fantasies of these men begin and end in loneliness. If I was paid to keep them company, then it was not for me to mock their dreams, because for them it was all deadly serious. I had seen enough to know that we prostitutes help society to let off steam, but no one thanks us for helping prevent explosions.

So I must not describe the Professor's interests in a disparaging way, although I was not really in sympathy with them.

After a time I got to know what he wanted, and everything ran to his satisfaction. All I basically had to do was read from the Old Testament, which seemed to me to reveal a harsh and vengeful God. But it was essential to my role to commit childish "sins". One time I tottered to my Bible class in high heels. I thought they looked silly with my school uniform, but the incongruity inflamed the Professor, who then made me pick up the shoes in my mouth and take them to him. He snuffled lingeringly at them and finally threw them to one side. I am familiar with these sublimated forms of sadism, masochism and fetishism, but the particular scenario brought some new surprises every time.

On other occasions I left some of my blouse buttons undone, and the professor would then rebuke me for it with pious solemnity, his face congested with the strain.

"Wretched wench, thou knowst not what prodigal gifts nature has lavished upon thee. Thou art yet but a child, put this fleshliness from thee!"

Then I would have to set to work on another heavy text from the Bible.

I would always be told off for sitting in an immoral position.

"Do not part thy legs in sin, my child! Pull down the hem of thy skirt!"

I decided to hot things up a little the next time we met by wearing no knickers and sitting with my legs quite shamelessly apart. He nearly went out of his mind.

"The dark carbuncle of womanly sin is come upon thy childish loins! Oh woe!"

That was heavy stuff. How much further could I take it?

I could not resist trying it on again. The next time I had shaved away my pubic hair, and happily announced:

"Now I am a child of Jesus once more!"

It may not have had much to do with the Old Testament, but at least it was Christian . . .

That is all I will say about the Professor, because I am in danger of losing myself in a subject that I only really understand in terms of Buddhism – sex and religion. But I will tell you more about some other clients who manage to combine religiosity with their sexual desires.

One of them is C.B., who comes from a rich Hanseatic family and lives in a rambling villa overlooking the Elbe. As he is the sole heir to his family fortune his privacy is invaded at weekends by other members of the family who want to be remembered in his will. His only company the rest of the time comes from his gouty old chauffeur, who comes to collect me in an ancient Mercedes 300, and his unsmiling housekeeper, a fossil of a woman.

When I visited this customer for the first time I was invaded by a strange sense of unreality. It had been a day of rainy squalls coming over the city from the North Sea, and now great black clouds were drifting across the evening sky, while rain dripped from the sombre copper beeches in the grounds of the house. The elaborate Jugendstil facade of the house hardly looked welcoming. It seemed strange, out of place, even threatening.

I expected the house to be cold and damp inside, but great

waves of heat and incense-laden air flooded over me. The gaunt housekeeper led me to a dark, vaulted room and closed the door silently behind me. The smell of incense was over-powering, and at first my eyes were confused by all the candles and "everlasting lights" scattered around the room. On a bier in the middle lay an open coffin made of heavy and gleaming black oak lined with white satin. It was floating on an ocean of deep red long-stemmed roses, whose fragrance penetrated through the incense as I got closer. Suddenly Gregorian chants began to echo through the crypt.

I had to get ready for the show. I had listened to what the customer wanted during previous conversations, and I hoped that I would look the part. I put on bra and pants made of smooth white silk. I had ripped both items of underwear a little, to make it look as though I had been victim of an act of violence, and I had painted a red stain at the crotch. I lay down in the swathes of cool satin, folded my hands over a single rose and lay still, trying to breathe as inconspicuously as possible, and with one of my thighs turned slightly outwards, so as to create the impression of a defiled corpse frozen in rigor mortis.

A slight draught prickled the hairs on the back of my neck, and I knew that the old man had come in. I nearly began to shudder uncontrollably. I felt so vulnerable, not ready for the responsibilities that were being loaded onto me. I belonged in another continent, where I understood people's needs and fantasies, ones which could be expressed in simple terms. Here I seemed to be taking everything onto my shoulders. All my clients were successful men in the eyes of society, who were able to move in the highest circles. But I was the one who had to guide them over to the dark and private side of their lives, the home of their terrible and despairing dreams and obses-sions. I knew the inner urges that drove them to public success, I had the key to the understanding of the aggressive motivation of life here. It was my vocation to ferry them

across the Styx, to the land of their true existence where their
longings could be fulfilled. Here a man could take revenge on
the mother who had not loved him by both loving and hating
her in the form of a harlot. Here he could strike the sceptre
from the hand of the overbearing father he had hated, and in an
eternal exhibition of triumph he could brandish his own. This
fantasy world may have been real for them, but I did not
belong there! How could I keep taking these journeys to the
realm of Hieronymous Bosch?

As the chants echoed around in the dome of the crypt, I
heard a whimpering and moaning on my left. It was in the
broken falsetto tones of an old man. I was glad to hear this
voice, because it meant that the terrifying death wish, the
fantasies of necrophiliac union, were merely the product of the
imprisoned imagination of a pitiful man. And my sense of pity
gave me strength. It was the only sentiment open to me, and it
brought me back to reality. I even felt a certain sense of relief
for the old man, when he finally signalled his fulfilment with a
hoarse cry.

Another of my clients, a figure in political life, has secret
transvestite leanings. He likes to come round to dress up and
put on make-up. I have reserved part of my wardrobe for
"her". Strangely enough an almost woman-to-woman
friendship has grown up between us, as I sometimes realise
with a touch of amusement.

"She" is as vain as a peacock, and never tires of having me
admire "her" in an endless array of clothes. Recently "she"
even spent the evening of "her" birthday with me – although
his wife and children were waiting at home. I helped "her" to
dress up particularly seductively that evening, because I had a
little surprise in store. I suggested we go out for an Italian
meal. "She" was very excited by the thought of being seen in
public. Just as we were about to start on our *antipasti*, a man I
knew came up to our table. I invited him to join us. Now, I
had let him in on the secret beforehand, and he played his role

181

with such passion that I had to keep running off to the loo so that I could burst into laughter there. They were behaving like a pair of lovebirds, and my friend finally got "her" to slip him "her" telephone number.

When we said goodbye at my flat "she" kissed me on both cheeks, and told me with a giggle that of course it was not a real phone number "she" had given him. "She" had spent a wonderful evening and was glowing with pleasure.

★

> *"I want no more soliloquies*
> *Between my restless fingers,*
> *And your garrulous thighs*
> *Between my fixed looks*
> *And your deceitful eye-shadow;*
> *And no more*
> *Between my loud, uncertain words*
> *And your hairy, swollen souls.*
> *I will take everything,*
> *Even the smell of my body,*
> *From your rooms.*
> *I will lay myself down*
> *In the junk that has long been silent,*
> *Listening to raindrops at measured intervals.*
> *I will paralyse myself with frost,*
> *And tire myself with heat.*
> *And watch the rust."*

I am lying in a snakeskin leotard on the black satin sheets of my bed. The canopy of the bed is arched over me. I have made a bamboo hut and planted a palm grove in pots around it. In the background soft, sentimental Thai music is playing, echoing

around. I stretch myself, open my legs, shamelessly displaying the vulva and anus like an animal on heat. I withdraw to
the darkest part of my bamboo hut, and relax there for a few
moments with a smile on my face. My client calls to me, stares
at me, looks down to his paper and writes a line.

I secretly call him "My poet". Outside in the real world he is
an important executive with all the trappings of success. But
here with me he is an impulsive and sensitive man. In his dim and
distant past a woman must have hurt him very badly, perhaps
his mother, perhaps someone he loved platonically, but she
must have shown cruel manipulation of sexuality to the young
man with his pubertal romantic dreams culled from literature.
He is torn between love and hate for women. He writes me
poems in an attempt to improve my literary education, but the
words he writes are bitter, angry and yet despondent. He
dedicates them to me by crumpling them up into balls and
throwing them at me. I read them out to him, reciting them
with chaste ceremoniousness like the goddess of art in the
Pantheon. Then I work at turning him on again until he comes
to a violent climax. I wipe the sweat gently from his face with a
damp cloth.

"The spiralling circles of pelts
Corrode away in the tireless leaden prattle.
The hulking Tower of Babel
Looms in the transfigured ferment.
And William Tell's convulsively panting bolt
Lurches around the hot stovepipe.
The opposites fall so madly for each other
That the caustic redness of love gnaws close to
    Q to the power of two.
All that will be past
When the primeval hag has taken the filth from her
    skirts

And the pubic pines have been cleared,
And the gorge has opened her thighs.
But first let the
Uterus burst like an overripe pomegranate."

In Buddhism the nun is shaven-headed and dressed in white; in Christianity she is wrapped in a shapeless black habit. But both are embodiments of mortification of the flesh and total detachment from things physical. They have eliminated all sexual desires, and become the antithesis of the whore – the saint. And yet how close the two can be.

Noi, my saviour in Khon Kaen was both the madame of a brothel and a nun. And in the wild fantasies of men the opposites become interchangeable. The more elevated and holy the image of the woman, the greater the underlying desire to break the taboo and desecrate the purity of the image.

My dressmaker is used to unusual requests, but she was at a loss for a moment when I asked her to make me a nun's habit. However, a dressmaker working in a red-light district knows as much about male fantasies as the girls do, and it did not take her long to get used to the idea.

M.R. is a real mummy's boy. He is heir to a lot of money which is still in his mother's hands. At first I found him spoiled, moody and blasé, but his facade crumbled as soon as he initiated me into his fantasies. At first they were inconsistent and misleading, sometimes directed at his strong mother, sometimes at his strict governess. I had the idea that he should make confession to a nun. To tell the truth, I do not know if a Catholic nun is allowed to take confession from a man, but my client was immediately very taken with the idea.

When M.R. is coming to see me, I powder my face white, put on red lingerie – really tarty stuff – beneath my habit, and make a confessional out of two screens. I put on a tape of organ music and place candles around the room. Then we begin an amusing little game. I think it makes him really happy, because I play readily along with him, and the threat of punishment, which lies deep in his lonely and overwhelming nightmare fantasies, loses its impact.

He whispers through the peephole, his voice full of emotion:

"Mother, I have sinned!"

"Confess your sin, my son. Was it unspeakable thoughts once again?"

"Yes, Mother. I have been tortured again by unchaste thoughts of your body."

Then he makes a litany of his sexual fantasies, and begs me to show him my body, and give him "a little holy image" of it as a devotional object. I hold up a cross to defy Satan, and then undress, slowly, stylishly, and quite obscenely.

★

At last the long nights and dreary days of the northern winter are over.

The May sunshine pours in past the plants and splinters in the woven bamboo over my bed, scattering points of lights over the dark silk.

Some of these little stars get caught in his thick brown hair and dance over the muscular contours of his shoulders and arms. They stroke the nape of his neck, and I cannot resist following their example. He growls like a teddy bear, and we snuggle up closer together. I like his smell. Images of the night return and tickle my newly refreshed senses. The air is cool, and the hairs on his body stand on end. I gently stroke them the wrong way. After more than two years of cold, drought and famine my body is once again sated with physical warmth, desire and sexual strength. It intoxicates me to know that I am free and strong, and yet full of love and devotion.

It must be about three months ago that I decided to seduce him. The sexual tug between us was in danger of being suppressed to the point of aggression. We had not said anything to each other to liberate our feelings. That was why I asked him over for dinner.

The table was ready and there was a fire burning. A storm was rattling the windows, making the scene inside look even cosier.

He shyly handed me a pretty little bouquet of flowers. At first he spoke in an uncertain voice, sometimes breaking into a silly giggle at the wrong moment. He was excited, I could tell. But then, I had made myself look nice for him. I wanted to capture him, and it was to be tonight. I was wearing high-heeled black boots, fishnet stockings, a plunging top with very thin straps. It was all in my own particular style, black, softly gleaming, and with a special simple elegance.

I had made a Chinese fondue, and the charcoal was glowing ready in the "steamboat". Eating this meal is slow and cere-monious, so it does not sit on the stomach or make you feel bloated. I did not want my plans spoiled.

There is hidden passion in Rioja wine. It blurs your vision a little, but does not prevent you from hitting the bullseye, as we discovered when we looked at each other after the first bottle. How I wanted him. There was a magnetically physical attraction.

I had been waiting for this night for two years,. Now I was at the spring in the oasis, drinking like a camel half-dead with thirst after crossing the desert.

I exploded in his arms like a box of firecrackers. My passion carried him with me, and together we sprang into the steam-ing cauldron.

The first time I had seen him he was carrying a large block of wood down the stairs. He was wearing a black vest, which showed off his smooth flesh and his athletic torso. I liked the look of him. When he came back up again I was suddenly looking into his brown eyes, which were dreamy yet bold. I felt a tickling at the back of my neck. Then he lowered his gaze.

I introduced myself, since he lived and worked in the basement of my block of flats.

I gradually found out from the other tenants that he was a sculptor, wood carver, painter, potter and designer. For all his versatility he had to work very hard to earn enough to live on. He often owed rent, and on Sunday mornings he would buy job lots of goods that were going off in the main hall of the market on the Fischmarkt. This meant he sometimes lived off overripe tomatoes for a week.

He had been a lecturer at an art college in south Germany, but had been dismissed for his radical views. He had condemned "elitist salon art" and had advocated a new kind of everyday art, which would be both passive, preserving the environment and in harmony with nature, and active, planning towns. He dreamed of a constructive ecological spirit in town planners, architects, road builders, traffic controllers, landscape gardeners, painters and designers. He wanted to make towns green again, fill them with colour, make them peaceful. He liked graffiti artists with their anarchistic spray cans, defying the brutality of concrete, and despised the fraternity which spent its time making chit-chat at exhibition openings, unable to see art as a passionate expression of emotions and life.

The more I heard about him, the more I wanted to get to know him better. I could tell that he was determined to keep out of my way, but at the same time I knew that he would appreciate an opportunity to behave differently. So why was he being so offhand? He probably thought I was just a spoiled high–class tart, that I would take advantage of his feelings. How could I find out what he really thought?

Then a terrible threat came over our block of flats. It had got into the hands of a property developer's which wanted to "gentrify" it and sell the place off as "luxury apartments". All the tenants had been given notice to leave. It saddened me to think of leaving the flat I had put so much into, but a sense of defiance rose up in me too. These feelings were shared by the other tenants attending our residents' meeting: the husband and wife teachers with all their children, the shopkeeper's widow, the sweet gay interior decorator, dear Herr Samuel, who in his old age had come back from Israel, the family of Vietnamese refugees, and all the others. A great sense of warm solidarity was felt by all the members of the residents' association, and we elected Kristoffer, the artist, to act as our spokesman to the new proprietors, though there was not much chance that the affair would come out in our favour.

But then it turned out that the property market was going through a bad time for sellers. Kristoffer called a residents' meeting one evening and announced excitedly that the developers had gone into bankruptcy.

"This is our chance! The receiver has told me that the building can be bought for nine hundred thousand marks. If we can get together a third of the sum as a deposit, then we could probably get a bank to give us a mortgage for the rest."

The residents were filled with hope – until they realised that, considering the financial position of most of them, they would never be able to get three hundred thousand marks together.

I had said nothing, shocked by the thought of what needed to be done. But I could raise half that sum if I sold my stocks and shares, and a bank would lend me the rest. I would never be offered such a large and well-kept block at such a good price again. My head was reeling as I thought things over. The rent would be enough to cover repayment and interest on a medium-term loan. I could set up a reserve fund and would even stand to make a profit.

I was thrilled to think that after eight years as a whore I was on the point of achieving my goal: permanent financial security. At fourteen years old I had been raped in Khon Kaen. Since then my only real dream was that one day I would no longer have to sacrifice my body to be able to live.

The sun was coming up, and I had been awake all night. But I now felt quite calm. I took a long bath and ate a hearty breakfast. Then I went off to the bank. They could not have been more obliging. The branch manager went with me to see the receiver. Soon everything was sorted out.

My feet seemed to find their own way home. Then I went down to Kristoffer's studio. There was such sadness in his face that I just wanted to hug him.

He was completely bewildered when I told him I was the new landlady.

"Everything's sorted out. Now you'll all be able to stay."

It made me so happy to see the loving look he gave me.

Then I asked him if he would be my caretaker with free rent and a small salary. That would allow him to carry on with his art without worrying where his next meal was coming from. I may have wanted him as a lover, but he was not going to be my kept man . . .

Then I asked him over for that Chinese dinner.

*

It was unusually hot that summer. I had bought a Volvo coupé, old but in very good condition, and we went on a lot of outings together.

We would often go on walks over the Elbe dyke to Fähr-mannssand. We spent a week in Juist, where we ran over the endless banks of sand down to the sea, holding hands with the wind in our faces. We tried to go from Dunen to Neuwerk by

189

going across the mud flats at low tide, but we finally turned back when we got to the third tideway. The current in the channel was just too strong for us. We also spent a few days on the little Danish island of Aerö, where we stayed in a sweet little guesthouse, whose roof was so low that you could reach it with an outstretched arm.

I have become a bit lazy these days, and have finished with some of the clients I liked less than the others. I no longer feel such a need to establish my freedom as a woman through achieving financial freedom. I will probably always be thrifty, but that does not mean to say I do not enjoy my creature comforts. For instance, Kristoffer and I love to go late at night to the Man Wah on the Reeperbahn and eat Cantonese *dim sum*, the little delicacies served in stacked-up baskets.

Kristoffer is now insisting more and more often that he should be the one to pay for the meal. The paradoxical principle I have always worked by is working for him. Now that he has financial security he can make himself sought-after as an artist. And the more choosy he is, the more money he makes. He also sometimes lectures on the role art has to play in ecology, and receives commissions from the university.

I am pleased that he is so interested in my work, although it does sometimes embarrass me that he regards it so highly. He even painted me a nameplate once, saying, "MALEE – Artist and Psychologist."

Next year I want to fly to Thailand with him. I so much want to see my family and Pim. It may still be dangerous for me there, at least in Pattaya, but I will get Kristoffer to go and search Pim out and bring her to me. Perhaps he will discover that she is in fact married and in Denmark. That would make me happy.

I do not know if I will go back to live in Thailand. I would not be much good farming rice. I have become too spoiled for that. Perhaps I will just stay here, or maybe divide my time between the two places. And I want to know if Kristoffer could ever consider living in Asia. My decision will not depend on him, but I would be happy if we could spend the future together, loving, yet free.

In a few days' time Kristoffer is having some friends round to celebrate my twenty-third birthday.

The typhoon has blown away the cocoon. The butterfly spreads its wings.